donAlphabetics

*An Adult Version of the Alphabet
A Humorous Description of America's
Situation under Dumbnald*

ADELE JAMES, BENTWORTH JAMES & CECI JAMES

Copyright © 2020 Adele James, Bentworth James & Ceci James.

All rights reserved. No part of this book may be used or reproduced by any means, graphic, electronic, or mechanical, including photocopying, recording, taping or by any information storage retrieval system without the written permission of the author except in the case of brief quotations embodied in critical articles and reviews.

This is a work of fiction. All of the characters, names, incidents, organizations, and dialogue in this novel are either the products of the author's imagination or are used fictitiously.

Archway Publishing books may be ordered through booksellers or by contacting:

Archway Publishing
1663 Liberty Drive
Bloomington, IN 47403
www.archwaypublishing.com
844-669-3957

Because of the dynamic nature of the Internet, any web addresses or links contained in this book may have changed since publication and may no longer be valid. The views expressed in this work are solely those of the author and do not necessarily reflect the views of the publisher, and the publisher hereby disclaims any responsibility for them.

Any people depicted in stock imagery provided by Getty Images are models, and such images are being used for illustrative purposes only. Certain stock imagery © Getty Images.

ISBN: 978-1-4808-9738-0 (sc)
ISBN: 978-1-4808-9739-7 (e)

Library of Congress Control Number: 2020919643

Print information available on the last page.

Archway Publishing rev. date: 11/09/2020

Contents

Dedication	vii
How It Started	ix
A	1
B	5
C	10
D	14
E	18
F	20
G	23
H	26
I	29
J	32
K	34
L	37
M	40
N	44
O	48
P	51
Q	57
R	59
S	63

T 68
U 72
V 75
W 78
X 82
Y 84
Z 86

Acknowledgments 89
About the Author 91

Dedication

The book is dedicated to our late parents: Anita Lestrade James and Benoit J. James.

You taught us the importance of using correct grammar and speaking proper English and fostered our love of reading.

We love you!

How It Started

Our family members live in different places: Dominica, Aruba, Barbados, New York, Massachusetts, the Netherlands, and the UK.

Over seven years ago we started a family group chat on WhatsApp. We use our chat to pray, share jokes, give birthday greetings, and talk about the news. Most of all, we talk politics.

When the quarantine started, there was lots of confusion, fear, and uncertainty and no clear message from the government, especially when it came to wearing or not wearing a mask. We used our family chat to check up on each other, cheer each other up, and give tips on staying healthy and safe.

Unfortunately, we lost our sister-in-law in London, who died of the coronavirus.

In spite of our grief, we used our family group chat to express our concern and sometimes anger while describing news reports. That was when someone used five words starting with the same letter!

The idea came up to use one letter of the alphabet to describe the day's current situation. We started with the letter A, and everyone submitted a sentence, a paragraph, or a story using the letter of the day. The following day was the letter B, and so on. This brought lots of laughter while we all tried to outdo each other, using words the others had never heard of. We used some French Patois, which is spoken in Dominica, St. Lucia, Haiti, and many other French Caribbean islands; some Papiamento, which is spoken in Aruba, St. Maarten, Curaçao, and the Netherlands; and some Jamaican slang.

Completing the alphabet took more time than expected, but by the time we got to the letter S we knew we had some humor to share with fun-loving readers.

Obviously, we needed to do some sanitizing before publication (hahaha).

We hope everyone finds something to enjoy in our book. Laugh out loud and relieve the stress that most of us feel during these times. We are all in this together.

donAlphabetics

---------- **1** ----------

America! America! Alas! Alas! You have been Abused by this Abomination called orange man. America is Angry, America is Ashamed!! Alice is Aching. What went wrong America? What happened Alice? Were you so Afraid And unsure about A woman President in 2016 that you And America voted for this Arrogant, Abusive, Abhorrent, Abnormal Authoritarian Asshole!! Hopefully, his Allies will Abandon him And leave him Ailing, Aching, And Angry. Now America And Alice Anxiously Await November 3rd, 2020 to vote for this Amazing, Awesome, Admirable, Authentic, Able and very *ALERT* Joe!! Y'all know Joe, the (sleepy one). Only then Alice's America will be Acclaimed, Abloomed, And Ameliorated And will scream Alleluia!! Alleluia!! We Are Alive And Auspicious Again!

---------- **2** ----------

Alas!! An Ape Assumed the office most Aspired for in America And since then the American dream has become unattainable. He is not Aware that he is An Ass - but everyone else has Attained that Awareness. He Acts like he is Almost God but Alas, his Actions Are Astoundingly Asinine, And his Attitude is Awful! He is An Anviege [1] Agitator. Stay Away from him!

After the Acute embarrassment that he Actively endured by Advising Americans to inject disinfectant, we can All hope And pray that he Acquired a lesson from All this. Ask Almost All Americans And they will Advise you not to Acquaint yourself with this Arrogant Ass. Always be on the Alert. Aah! Now the Anti-Trump Campaign has picked the Aspiring Joe/Kamala Association to run Against him.

3

Are you ready for Award winning donAlphabetics? Once Again! Are you ready? Are you sure? Anou Allez! [2] America's Annoying orange Absent-minded Award-winning A-Hole is Alarming Adverse. It is so damn Absurd, Agonizing And Appalling to know that this Abusive and Abrasive Abomination who Accidentally became A head of state, doesn't Absorb Air, he Admires And Angrily Accuses Amazon's CEO, Aggravates the Atmosphere, And Abnormally drinks A glass of Aquafina H2O. So Apathetic like he just drank Acid. This Adulterous, Almost-Aborted, pre-Arrival Ailment Always Angrily Abuses Any And everyone in An Atrocious Abrupt manner. He Acts like there Are no Adults in his Administration, so he Arbitrarily Attacks his non-Admirers, An Annihilation to Authority, and Afraid to Associate with fruits and veggies. Such An Appalling, Abysmal, Anxious Addicted-to-Assness orange Ape. He Acts like he is still on his Antiquated Apprentice. America is Ashamed & Abashed with this Allergic horse crap. Abandoning, Abaseing, And displaying Abhor to our

---

[1] Anviege (French Creole) – greedy (especially for money and tangible possessions)
[2] Anou Allez (French Creole) – Let's go

donAlphabetics 3

Allies while Abiding with, And Assisting All dick-tators, FOX, Alex Joness and oAn.

Always engaging in Adhoc Adventurous Algorithms while stashing America's Assest in his Attic before definitely being Asconded in November. Please America, I'm up in Arms Asking, Ail up All your Allies, sound the Alarm: Antigua, Arkansas, Arizona, Aruba, Afghanistan, Anse du May, Argentina, Alaska, Ayola And All our Australian Aborigines ... Aylas Bondiay[3]. ... he must Accidentally Annihilate himself with his Automated Assault AR15.

This orange Animal must be Abandoned. Acting like America forgot that he Absolutely has to be Audited. His American Audience expresses total Apathy with his constant Aspersion. Awkward Authority on America, Admonished by All, he stands Arbitrarily, His Accolades are Atrocious. I'm Awaiting with Appreciation for his twitter App to Abate. Zero Amicability, total Adverse, Animosity And Askance, his lies Are so Audacious And Abusive. Idiot's Articulation Appraisal is Awful, not Awesome. Terrible with his ABC's, can't remain Attentive And Always Ad-libing. He Argued with April Rian last August, he is Anti Anthony Fauchie, Accused And Ambushed Jim Acosta, Aggravated And Agonized Allyson Camarota, now he is Against Anthony Kenneddy, Attacked And Annoyed David Axelrod. Who the hell tells a news reporter that "you're Always Asking questions?" While Actively Assaulting our Allies, this Airhead deliberately uses Ad hominem And Anecdotal Fallacy in his Awful mouth opening sounds. Not At All Appropriate and very Abominable. This Abstract, Absent minded Adulterer Always Assists in Atrocious and Abhorrent Assnesses (plural). He is Acrimoniously Ambushing the Post Office to Agony with his Appalling suggestions. Absence And Atrocious crowd At Ailing rallies, Assumed he is A billionaire, Apallingly self-Alleged that he is human, An Authentic American A-Hole! An Apathetic

---

[3] Aylas Bondiay (French Creole) – Oh God!

Autocrat, he Aggressively Autographed An Alabama weather map, He cannot Add An Apple And An Apricot, He Acclaims it's Algebra. An Antagonistic bully with no cupid Arrow of Affection with Melanie, she And her Aggravating Asinine "Be Best BS", with her Alligator purse And Accessories. Anguish Against Absentee ballots, Allergic to Apologize, Affirmatively Anti-Black, he Altered BLM to ALM, but before he And his Anarchistic mAgA goons Accompany Americans to An Apocalypsetic Agony, Dr. Az should Amputate the Annoying Abscess from his Aimless Annoying Assbrain, located in the Approximate Area of his Ailing Asshole ... Allez Akai ou, pandi![4] America is Angry ...

Ah Ah Ah Ah Ah ... Aylas[5]

---

[4] Allez Akai ou, pandi (French Creole) – Go home, you worthless
[5] Aylas (French Creole) – Oh oh

donAlphabetics

B

1

Boy mister is a real Boowoe[6]! But wait!! Break-Break-Breaking news. His Best Buddy Banion just busted today. Doing Borball[7] with Borderwall Bucks. Living Big! He is already claiming Baselessly there will Be Borball[8] this election. Billy, Bush, Boston, Brison. Whatever Badass name you give yourself. Be Bold and vote Blue or you will end up like Bubba your Black Buddy. But there's a Bigger story about to Break. That Bastard, Bombastic Bore Bilton. His Book is a Bestseller, But Both he and orange Buffon were Best Buddies at one time. Now they are Bickering like two Bitches.

But now Byden has his slogan Build Back Better or Better Build Back Big. Sleepy Boy is out of his Basement!

That Buffon is also trying to Block another Blasting, Blistering Book. Blaming and Bashing for his Brother's Bereavement. Boy oh Boy!! I heard that Dumbnald has another hidden secret

---

[6] Boowoe (French Creole) - Bastard
[7] Borball (French Creole) - Fraud
[8] Borball (French Creole) - Fraud

B-child!! Look Bacchanal! It is Baffling that this Barefaced, Bizarre, Bigheaded Bigot has not Been Blasted away to his Baby Bunker Bed, where we will sing Bye Bye Bunker Boy, go suck on your Big Bloody Boo Boo.

2

Bondiay[9] That Big Brazen Boastah[10] racially- Biased Black Bison is Basically on our Backs! He is not mentally Balanced But he is Big on calling other Beings Bad names. He himself looks like a Bug with a Bobo.[11] He is a Bad Bossy Bitchy Bloated Bigot with a Big head, Big Butt, and Boarlike Behavior.

The Boy likes to play Badass But Basically has no Backbone. His Businesses are all Broke But he claims to have Bank with his Broke-ass self. Bomboclatt[12] Bwai!! [13]

Blaming his Bummed rally on protesters. Bugger! He shouldn't have had the Blasted rally in the first place. What a Bloody mess! Best mister has stayed his Butt in his Bed.

Before his next Birthday we Bound to Boost that Baboon Back to his Bunker. He does not Belong in the Beautiful (White) House. Boom! Boom! Boom! Let's Blast him Back to where he Belongs.

3

Boy Boy oh Boy ... I am Badly Baffled By this orange Backward Backbiting Bum who cannot Brainstorm and stay focused in

---

[9] Bondiay (French Creole) – O God
[10] Boastah (French Creole) - Boastful
[11] Bobo (French Creole) – an ugly wound
[12] Bomboclatt (Jamaican English) – Swear word similar to "shit" and "fuck"
[13] Bwai (Jamaican Patois) - Boy

daily WH Briefings. This Bankrupt Barbarian got no Balls. Busy to reopen Businesses then gets Busted. His Blueprint is not legible. He is a Bashful Bastard with a Big Bobo[9] Brain. He visited Britain But Boris and Big Ben didn't Blink. He had to ride at the Back of the Bus. That Barbaric Beast is always Bashing and Broadcasting some BULLSHIT like wanting to Buy Greenland. Boooo!! Biggest fan of Braxton Brag. Boooo!!He must be Banned from Breathing, unless it's carbon dioxide. He should Be the one Bawling: "I can't Breathe, I can't Breathe". He is a Brutal, Bloated, Bogus, Boastful, Boisterous, Bratful, Bigass, Ballheaded BIATCH. Always Begging for praises while Belittling others. Bitch Be like ... Badly Broke, not a Billionaire like Mike Bloomberg. So damn Belligerent, a damn Bragging Bullneck. His Bandwidth is Broadband Bacteria, no Bueno. This Bigot is Bad with English. Baffles Brook Baldwyn, and Basically off-track to Blitzer's understanding. He and his Beer drinking Buddies Brett Kavenar and Bill Bahr took Bets on who Backbites, Bank-frauds, Betrays and Borbols[14] Better. Brazen like Barracudas. Disrespected BLM and Bubba Wallace. That's why he Banned Blacks from his Buildings in the Burroughs or Bronx and Brooklyn. Only Black he likes is his Black Bullying sharpie. He tries to Bully Byden, fear of Byden Building Back Bolder and Better!

Boowoe Blanc sala[15] has Bad Behavior. Bob the Builder is way Better! Bondiay pas Behniei.[16] Came up with some Bone spurs Bullcrap on Both feet. President Brainspurs told Deborah Byrx some Bullshit aBout Bleach, he and his Baseless claims ... Basic BS! He still uses Breeze to wash his Briefs and Boxers. Bill Mahhar thinks this Brat a Big Baby.

Big Byrd got a Bigger Brain than this Bipolar Bank Frauder. He is Beneath Presidential dignity with his Bogging Bullshit. Beaviis &

---

[14] Borbol (French Creole) - Bribe
[15] Boowoe blanc sala (French Creole) – This white good for nothing
[16] Bondiay pas Behniei (French Creole) – God didn't bless him

Buttthead could do a better job than Pence and this Bad hombre with his mob Boss Body language and this no Beauty, Beyond the plate Behavoir. This Bone Spurs Buffoon thought Best Buy sells Bread, Butter and Bleach. Barbel Blew up and Broke up when he asked to translate: "How do you say I'm the Best President in Bullshit, Bankfraud, Bullcrap, Bribery, Bankruptcy, Belittleing, Betrayal, Blaming, Bitter and Blasphemy?"

He got a Bullseye to Betray people in his Bogus Businesses. He is not Bright Because he doesn't read Books. Black Lives Matter ka Boolay chooi[17], Boowoe Sa-a pa Belle[18], E say un Buick.[19] He should Be kept in a Brown Broken Beaten-down Barn.

Even Baron Begged him to Bring Back oBbama, so he called Baron a Bastard, then he told Baron, Byden is your Boepere.[20] What a Big Baby! 911 ... calling for a Black Babysitter! We know he sleeps wearing Melanie's BIG Busted Burgundy Bras. Whenever he calls her Baby or Babes, she responds: "Hi Brainless". He should start eating some Bigtime Banana Braff[21] while listening to Aka Banton's Bouyon. Bigup Bigup! Led kon Boos, plis led parsay Booboo.[22] E ka ani Bavay sot[23], starting his oBama Berthir BS. E ni Bouche.[24]

Secret Service Code name: 6B. BIG Busted Bobo Bottom-Brained BITCH!! I'm hoping Bermuda, Bahamas, Barbados, Belize, Brazil & Great Britain Ban him from visiting. Don't Bring your crap here Boy! Get me some Bug spray! Be gone Boldface! Your Band didn't

---

[17] Boolay chooi (French Creole) – Burning his ass

[18] Boowoe Sa-a pa Belle (French Creole) – this good for nothing is not beautiful

[19] E say un Buick (French Creole) – He is a donkey

[20] Boepere (French Creole) - Stepfather

[21] Braff (French Creole) - Broth

[22] Led kon Boos, plis led parsay Booboo (French Creole) - Ugly like a puffer, uglier than a blowfish

[23] E ka ani Bavay sot (French Creole) - He just dribbles nonsense

[24] E ni Bouche (French Creole) - He has obea

play any Bouyon, Bachata or Bad Bunny at your inauguration, U Bitch. But Brace yourself! Holding up a Black Bible in front a Burnt church won't save you from a BIGLY Brutal Byden Beating! ... like you fell from a Balcony onto a pile of Bricks. You Buckled Brain-damaged BASTARD!! "How did I fall off this Balcony? It was a Beautiful Balcony. The Biggest, Boldest, Brightest, most Balanced Balcony anyone has ever seen. No one has seen anything like that, No one has seen anything like that, Bravo!"

donAlphabetics

C

1

This Corrupt Clown has failed the Citizens, as Corona Cases are rising and Congress Cannot Control him. He is Clueless, not Clever, and runs the Country like his Crime syndicate. It is Crystal Clear that he is not Capable of Controlling the Chaos, instead he Creates it. He has no Compassion. Man, Come on! You Cheated in school, you Cheated on your wives, you Cheated your Charity, you Cheated the tax man, and then you Cheated your way to Commander in Cheat! You and your Circle are full of Conmen and Criminals. You Could not Care a rat's ass about anyone but yourself. We Can't wait for the Culmination of this Clueless Clown to Cut the Crap and get his Caliginous face out of Circulation. To be Clear, mi ta hopi Cansa!![25] So ban Caba cu e Con Man na November.[26]

---

[25] Mi ta hopi cansa (Papiamento) – I am very tired
[26] So ban caba cu e con man na November (Papiamento) – So let's finish that con man at November

2

Compahwayzon! [27] Can you believe this Commander-in-Chief really thought he Could lead this Country? He does not Care about the average Citizen. He only Cares about Cash, his Comfort and Choo pool * with Common people. Couldn't handle Covid-19, Certainly Couldn't keep his Cool during the Civil unrest. Instead he Creating more tension among Civilians. What a Complete C*nt!! He is a Cheaply Colored Clown, Clueless Concerning Constitutional Content.

Americans' Confidence in him has Certainly been declining Considerably fast. Which should Clear the way for Biden to Come and Cwayvay[28] him in November. Castigates anyone who Challenges him. He Cannot run the Country. He is not Capable of Controlling his own life, far less for Common people's. He is a Crappy, Conniving, Crazy, Careless, Callous, Crooked, Cheating, Corrupt, and Childish Con artist.

Call me Crazy but I think this Cow should be Castrated for all the Crimes that he has Committed against women and Americans in general. Cut it off! Cut it off!! Clap Clap Clap!!

3

CAUTION!! Have you ever seen a Cheaper Catastrophic Cannibalistic Cheater? This Criminal is always in some Cumbersome Casualty-Causing Carnage and always in a Calamity like Carla from California. Talking about California, he Couldn't Comprehend California's Climate Conditions Changes, and now the Casualties and Colossal failure from the Current Circumstances.

---

[27] Compawayzon (French Creole) - Conceited
[28] Cwayvay (French Creole) - Beat

Taking a Closer look: He Capsized America with Corona, he Caused Chaos with COVID, always in a Careless Chatter with Confederate flag and Candyce Owens BS, lacks Common sense, and totally Clueless like he won the Cash-strapped Challenge. He is so Cursed that he has no Character. This Con artist is always in a Consistent Covfefe Controversy by avoiding Checks and balances. He hates Calypso and Callalou. Loves China China China! I saw him enjoying Curried Cat Cold Cuts in Chinatown. He was convinced it was Chicken.

Because his capacitors are overheating, and his Circuit breaker keeps tripping, he brought out his Calvary on peaceful Crowds Calmly and Cautiously Converging during Corona/Covid.

Charlotte the Crackhead, a Call girl from Club Capricorn in Corpus Christi, Considers him to be a Certified Creep. She Claims the way he Crawled up to her Contemplating some sorta Cruel Conductive analysis was definitely nothing to Celebrate, but Certainly Clear off, Cut & Run.

He is like a Chronic Callous Cancer. When he Coms, nothing but Compressed farts Come out. He's been Called Childish, the way he Clumsily walked down a Constructed ramp, he Claims it's his Cheap shoes BS. Chrys Cuomo & Anderson Couper think he's a Conman with a Corrupted CARES Act. Consequences be dammed! Can't Consume H2O under any Circumstance. Like a Culpable Conformist Cowboy, Condoned Flynn, Stone & others. What a Cunt! I hope he Chokes next time he eats Cowfoot and Cooked Catfish in a Calabash. His Covert Circles are Careless and Corrupted with Cupidity. A day without Crime and Controversy doesn't exist, Count it in. Always in a Chaotic Conspiracy theory with his Cartoonish lies. Terrible at Counting inauguration Crowds. This Contemptible Casualty hates CMN because they Criticize his Constant Convenient lies and his Catastrophic China virus multiple Centuplication. This Constipated Clot must Correct his Cyber Criminal behavior like Cutting CDC funding, and other Cold blooded Cancer Causing Conditions, that's why America is Caught in this Cataclysmic downturn. This outta Control Caveman is so difficult to Construe, always Chastising people and he loves Controversy.

Chumb's Colossal Cognitive difficulties and his existing Comorbidities has this Clod acting and looking like he is Certainly Constipated. That's why at a stopover in Cuba on his way to Carnival in Castries, someone came up to him saying, "Sir, you're Clearly kinda sorta Chubby, and your existing Comorbidity analysis Certainly indicates that you are suffering from a Circuit Clot in your Cranium. You should go on a Crystal-Clear diet of Celery, Cauliflower, Chard, Carrot, Cabbage and Citrus". This Cretin Claims that since Corona/Covid his Covenant is to Concentrate on Continuing Complex Cognitive Calculations like person, woman, man, Camera, tv.

E say un Cochon.[29] If he was in the Caribbean, he would be Called a vieux Carwant[30] but when Calendar hits Nov 03, this Compost pile's Childish Cock will be Castrated in a Civilized Censored Constructive manner. U Concur?

---

[29] Esay un Cochon (French Creole) – He is a pig
[30] Vieux carwant (French Creole) – Old ragamuffin

donAlphabetics

---- **1** ----

This Damn fool Don is DOMINATED BY THE DEVIL! A Dangerous Deceitful Demon, who brought Death and Destruction to such a Darling Delightful country. He is Deceitful and Dangerous and his son Donnieboy is a real Douchebag. Does nothing but tweet Despicable and Destructive messages. A bunch of Disgusting Dotards. Even our Dear sistah Donna in Dominica knows that Don is a Democrat in Disguise and is Determined to Destroy the Repubs!! So, let's Dump Don in the Deep Deep hole of Despair, because he is already Doomed to Damnation and Destruction!!

---- **2** ----

He is a Dumb, Dunce, Disgusting, Devilish, Disdainful, Damaging, Disgraceful, Disorderly, Dipsy, Dipshit, Dickheaded Dog. Definitely a Dufus and a Dolt.

donAlphabetics 15

Donald Dump Doh[31] know how to deal with Decent Democrats. He is a Dangerous Dog that is Doing nothing but Damaging the reputation of De[32] U.S. He is Dumb, Dotish and Definitely Desperate. He will Destroy anyone who Doesn't agree with his Dirty Disgusting behavior.

Lord Deliver us from this Devil! Don't let Americans Decide to put that Dude back and cause Dilemma! His Damaging behavior will have Drastic effects! This is not a Dream!

He says he Doesn't Drink - why Does he always act like he is Drunk?

Dump that Damn Dog in the Deep blue sea!

3

Damn Dumbnald! ... sorry, my bad, Damn Deceptive DumbnalD ... Daaats better. Dis is DonAlphabetics: D-Day. I am Dynamically Delivering a Deserving, Descriptive Dashboard, which Developed people Did with Dutiful Devotion, During the Dog Days of Disgusting Deceitful Dumbnald. What A Damn Dirty Dangerous Damaging Demonic Dump! Here is the Damage Report: This Diarrhea- Distributing Defective Delinquent Devil is like Damaged goods. A Dotish[33] Disgraceful Dick with Drunk-type Diction because the Diodes in his brain are Destroyed. Always Defaming, Dividing and Delegitimizing over Data from Deborah Byrx, Doctors & the CDC. Douchebag Dumbnald T starred in the failed movie "Deaf, Death, Dumb & Destruction" (D4 for short).

---

[31] Doh (French Creole) – Doesn't
[32] De (French Creole) - The
[33] Dotish (French Creole) - Stupid

This Divvy tells people he has Development in Dublanc, he Damn lie, Den he said: "U heard Dublanc, but I said Dubai". Damn lie again. Always Dealing in some Dirty Dishonest Dollars. Deliberately Denigrating people with his Deceitful behavior. Dumdbald, you are officially the Dumbest person in the Developed Diaspora. You've been Diagnosed as a Desperate and Dangerous Dolt. Dumdum Delivers Death to Democracy. His Deplorable and Disagreeable Discussions is like Death by 1000 cuts. This Dumbbell Disgusting Dies in Disturbing Defiance.

When Described by Dominant Democrats as a DAMASS, listen to him: "Hear Dat, hear Dat, A Damass calling a Damass Damass ... "What a DAMASS!! "Art of the Deal" was more like "Ass of a Deal", no big Deal. Not even a best seller at "Dumb & Dusty book Depot". Because Dunderhead is so Dumb, Dehumanizing & Disgusting, he tried to Drop Dacca to stop Dreamers.

What a Douchebag! His Dad tried Dumping his Dumb ass in a Dirty Dumpster, then he left him in a Dark Derelict building previously Discarded by Dennis Dubois from Delray Dunes, prior to a Demolition. Dat Depleted multiple-Divorced Dickhead is Dauntingly Distracted and Driving America in a wrong Direction. He Disrespects Donn Lemon and Daniel Dayle, but he worships Daved Duke. Defensive against Social Distancing with his Declining and Decaying polls.

Deliberately Delays and always in a Delinquent Deficit that banks in Detroit Declined his Deposits. Oh Dead! Dora the explorer is way more Developed. I think he's Drinking the wrong Drugs. Despites liquor but always looks Drunk and Disorderly, soon he will be in Deadbolt custody. We know that he reads in Darkness and he cannot Dance to a Drumbeat. Though people Demonstrate Dat he is Dropped Dead Dis election, he is still Defiant and getting more Defensive and Delirious. He even tried to Delay election Date.

Dumbmald must visit Darcia's Delight in Dominica to Digest some of her Delicious Decaffeinated Delicacies while Defrosting Da Dung in his headless Department. But Damn, he is a Dangerous Deadbeat, he will Defraud Darcia, and Dangerously Drop her into Debt. Her Development will Decrease & Decline! Darcia's sister Debbie will have to Depend on Donations! Deadbeat will Dangle the Dough but Don't Deliver! Dat Deceitful Dog. Dipstick's Demonstrably Discrediting false claims are Displeasing and Distasteful. His Distraction intent are Detestable because this Damn Donkey Dreadfully Doesn't understands the English language. Over 231K people Dead, but while Developing Distractions and Distruction, Dimwit is Defiant that "it will Disappear". He's so Despicable and Desensitized! Dis Dummy thought that Dawn Ultra was a Diverse stripper from Club Double D in Delmar, Delaware. Dat Dope Didn't pay his Dowasko and Domlek bills since Deotherday sometime last December. He Deliberately Didn't pay it Due to the fact that he was busy getting Dirt on Hunter, while Disassembling Obamacare. Due to his Deplorable and Disgraceful lack of Decency and Dignity, he has Developped self-inflicted Damage. He is a confirmed Dumbass but Do you Doubt that this Damass-in-Chief is Deaf and Deliberately Does Distructive and Deceptively Dangerous Deals to Darken and Dampen his Defectiveness?

Darcia will Drop him like a Dirty habit. DAYSAN! DIAB![34] So he will Daykarlay[35] and that Douchebag will get buried in a Deep Dark Ditch, Dug up by Dirty Devils like Don jr and Deryck Chauvyn. Death to Dat Dangerous Delusional Dog. A new Day is Dawning!

---

[34] Daysan diab (French Creole) – Go down! Devil
[35] Daykarlay (French Creole) - disassemble

donAlphabetics

---- **1** ----

Everyone thought he was the lesser of two Evils. Now it's time to Eradicate this Erratic, Evil, Exhausting Enemy of the people. An Eyesore with no leadership Experience. Exaggerating on Every issue. Ever heard of Tax Evasion? End that!

Eager to open churches for Easter pretending to be Evangelical. Does not Even care how many people die. Erasing Everything that Obama did with complete disregard for the Environment. This Eerie Egoistical Embarrassment of a so-called leader needs to End now.

---- **2** ----

This Egotistical Egg-headed, Embattled Eel is Exhausting, Energy-draining and Embarrassing. He is an Excessive Executive with Excrement Everywhere.

Even Early in the day Everyone didn't Expect him to Excel. But he Evidently has not Exceeded the Expectations of his Enemies.

Except for some he is Exactly the Embarrassment that he was Expected to be. Enjoying the presidential Experience quite Excessively while Expressing his lack of Expertise in performing his duties. His limited Education is Evident in the ways he Expresses his opinions at the wrong time. I think Everyone who has had Enough of this Executive should Express that Explicitly. Enough!!

---------- **3** ----------

This Envious Epidemic is an Extreme Extravagant Eyesore. He is Explicitly Explosive and needs to be Exterminated and Extinguished. His Equalizer needs some Equality tweaking. He is hated by Everyone, that's why he narrowly Escaped because of the Electoral College. An Expired Extremist who Extorts and Expunges Everyone and Everything with his Errors. Past Empathetic Presidents are Embarrassed. He is Exhausted, always Evolving in Expired Excuses. Egghead thought Earth Wind & Fyah was an East coast hurricane. Eeew! He spends Executive time in Enemy territory with his Exhuted Excruciating Exercises. Always on the Edge like he's Expecting an Eclipse. Enrique, Eduardo and Emanuel from El Salvador are his Everlasting Enemies. The medical Electrician who wired him wasn't Exclusive because he is an Evildoer. His Eggs were rotten, Embryo never developed. Look at Eric! They should all be put in Eternal Exile for Ever with no Escape.

donAlphabetics

---------------- **1** ----------------

This is a Fake, Fat, Flabby Failure who loves Forgiving eFFing criminals and Fabricating Falsehoods. He Is Furious that the American people Follow Dr. Fauci's guidelines and not his. He is Fascinated with Flattery and his Fans will Foolishly Follow him to his Finish. Doesn't his face remind you of someone who Forever has Flatulence? I heard he Farts while he tweets.

---------------- **2** ----------------

Orange is Fat, Fraudulent, Fucked up, Feces-Face Fool. He is a Fraudster who Fumes Formaldehyde and is Fashioned for Fake tv.

Family of this orange-Faced Fool should be embarrassed to Face the public. He Festers Fraudulence but accuses others of being Fake. He is False! His whole Fucking life is a Facade! He puts Fame and Fortune ahead of the needs and Feelings of the people. Not even Fearful of being Found out. His Finances are Fickle and he Frustrates the people by not revealing his yearly Financials. I am Fed up with this man! Frankly I Feel that he should Fall Flat on his Face!

3

This is not Fake news like Fox & Friends. Forty-Five (45). OMG what a Fraud, what a Fool! Forty-Four (44) was Forty-Five times better. This Failing Faithless FakAss President Faulty Fascist who happens to be a Fatty, Fearful, wanted-by-the-FBI Felon, is consistently involved in a Filthy Fiasco like Falking his Favorite daughter. Figure it out! He's made Famous by his Fraudulent Father Fucking up his Family. He Frequently Falks the First Lady, as per Fact checking. He Fabulously Freaked out France, Finland, Friends and Foreigners with his Flabbergasted Fuckeries.

Every Friday btwn 5:15 & 5:55 he Finds himself doing some Fucked up Fings. This False Figurehead Flagrantly Flares out his Flaws, Fights and Flirts with Falsehoods cleaning and raking the Floors of the California Forest to prevent Flammable Fires like they do in Finland.

Then he started his Fictitious Fifteen covid cases to 0 Fake news on his Favorite Fred Flintstone type Fox & Friends, Freaking out Fauchi, then echoing some Frank Rizzoo crap ... when the looting/ shooting. This Fool is not Fast but Fucking Furious like a Firery Furnace. Franceska Fiorentino said: "Frankly, like a Firstgrader, he cannot Figure out Facts". This Fat Fool is Forbidden to be reelected. Four more years? Yea right! In a Flimsy 4x4 Formica Frame on Frikers Island, U Freak!

He got Fired From the Financial & Fiscal Firm "Fried & Fisher". He Fucked up a French Fries Franchise, Failed a Flying company, Fooled his Friends and Frontline workers, still Faking his Followers in Florida, Failed a Fish & Fresh Fruit market because he loves

Fast Food. Both Farron and Fallon reported that last Friday, this Fool was given Fire trucks to play with Five year old Friends. Figure this out!

He wanted to File for insurance after the Florida Floods, but Flo told him to "Fuck off FuckFace!" With all the Flare-ups in Florida, Foreskin Falsely comes up with Falsehoods and Fake Figures like he did with his Fundraising and Fly-the-coop Finances, as per Fact checkers. Fathead is so Full of Farts. For a while, he was Feeling covered with his Foul, "Fine people on both sides" Fiction. Then he started throwing Foolish Flames that "Fauchi threw a Fifty mph Foul Fastball". Pure Forkeries. After being accused by Fifteen Females for his Fierce and Frightful Falsiloquence, he Forked up Farmers with his False tariffs on Fresh Fruits & Flowers. He is still Fixed on his Fort Brag & Fort Hood False Narratives. His Foes include FiftyFive Fishermen in Finland and a Few Fat Folks in Fatville. Now he's Fierce and Furious with the Feedback from his Favorite Fox news, so this Fool now calls them Fake Fox & Friends.

Americans have to Forget this Foul, Fraudulent, Flip Flopping Fuckface! Go Flush u Face, U Fat Fool ... you're Full of Forced Farts! Flies Follow you. Wear a Facemask! You're banned from Facebook. You're Fried, and You're Fired! Fuckoff 45!! Fuhgeddaboudit!! Finally, 44 was Fun, Faithful, Fabulous, Funky with Folklore, Famous with Family, Fans & Friends, Fantastic ... Freaking Funtabulous!

donAlphabetics

G

1

This Grossly, Grotesque, Greedy, P Grabber will go down as the Greatest,

Griping, Goon, ever!! He is Guilty of abandonment and Neglect of the American people. He is Garrulous, Gauche, and Gawky. Always has that Grandiose behavior. Gravitates to Dictators while he Grinds his Gargantuan butt away from our allies. Uses Goya for Gimmicks. We think before November 3rd he might quit due to Gastroduodenal issues.

2

Orange is a Greedy, Gross Gluttonous Girl (pussy) Grabber. His Grotesque Groin is like Garbage: Gonorrhea-Giving. A Gassy Geriatric Gargoyle who Grieves because he is not Great. His Giant Gangrenous butt keeps Growing so he needs to do Gymnastics.

Garcon[36] the presidency is not a Game! Give a Good Grade to the Great men who have Gone before you! You're too Greedy for Greatness. You need to Grow in Goodness. Give Generously! God will Grant you peace if you do. Go away, Gangster! Grrr!

3

President Garbage Goon is always Gaslighting some Gibberish. Geeez! This orange Goat is forever in a Gruesome Gripe, Grimacing, Gossiping and Grating with his Gangster-type Grammar, making America Great to the Gutter in the Ghetto. What Garbage people! He, Don the Grinch, GKush the Ghost and his other Greedy, Get-rich Grouches, always Gnawing and Goading some Gutless Grief. He is the head of the Grotesque Gold-robbing Gunmen. Groping flags, Golfing, Grabbing pussy and Gratifying Goya. This Grumpy, Gutless, Geezer Glaringly Grinds with his Gall, Garish, Gawking and Groundless Gripes. Genuine Governor Coumo was a much Greater and Graceful Gentleman. This orange President Grievance is always in some Gullible, Gutless, Greasy, GOP Grime. Goofus' Gift is Godawfully Gross and Glaringly Ghetto. Germen and Gerwomen from Germany Giggled at his Ghastly, Gabbling Gimmick. Glaringly Graceless and Gawky at G7 Group. Guests Got Giddy. Even GKush the Ghost Ghastly said: "This is Garbage I would Generally Get rid of, from my Gwam Girlfriend's Garage". This Guy didn't Graduate Grade school that's why he's not Good with Geography, Geometry, Geometrics and Gravity. Always has some Glitches and Grievances with Good people coming from Guatemala, Grand Bay, Grenada, Giraudel, Guyana, Grand Fond and Gambia. This Giant Manchild Got some Gruesome Grievances in regards to Greenhouse Gas emissions. Like he chewed on Goofy Garlic, there's Greasy Garbage in this Grim Gemini's Gut like "wishing Ghislaine well, it will Go away, Good

---

[36] Garcon (French Creole) - Boy

people on both sides, Gratifying Greg Gutfeld and lying on his Great Generals". So Goofy and Gruesome, always getting caught up in some Guilty Grudge, while Gainsaying with his Covid19 corrupt Genocidal Gimmicks. Like General Garbage, this Gauche Goof must Glide-be-Gone with his Golf buddies to his Grave this General election.

donAlphabetics

1

Humpty Donnie wanted a wall Humpty Donnie loves his beautiful wall. Hello!! It's easy to Hate this Hypocritical Hooligan. His Heinous Habits Has Helped His Hate filled Hostile and Harmful Heathens. He is even giving Heather a Headache!! But wait! Mexico did not pay for His Horrible wall. This country is going through Hardships, but His word of the day is Hoax! Hoax! Hoax! We hope this Harrison guy from the South will Humiliate them in November.

2

Hello!! This Horrible, Huge, Heavy, Hateful Hacker keeps Harassing Humans. He is Hungry for power and leaves his supporters Helpless. Old Hag. Always Has Half-assed ideas. How he got his Hair-thinning Heavy-handed self in the (White) House has me Humbly Hungry for information. He has a Hazy view on How to Handle the House. I am Horrified by His performance. Hope someone Hoists His ass out soon.

Humph, Hungry Hippopotamus! Heave your Horny Hips out of Here! Hollow- brained! You're no Hope for Hungry people!

3

Hello, Hello, anybody Home? How r U? Huh? Have you Heard? Huh? Hear dis!

This Hollow Hard-headed, Human tapeworm, President Horrible Hater is Heavily Harmful. He is a Heartless Hopeless Hazard, always creating Hideous Havoc. His Hate speech about Haiti, Havana and Honduras was even Hated by the Heads of Hitler's Hierarchy. He says Hateful things about Henry Hernandez and Herman Herrera from Hecho Gracias, Honduras. What a Horrible Hombre!

He is not a Healer, a definite Heartbreaker and Humiliator. He Hoards and Hijacks PPE, is Helpless to the First Responders and Helpful to spread Hate while he Hi-Fives Hostility. Always Hesitant to the truth and Hopeless to facts like when he was caught Hiding in the white House bunker with His Homies wearing their white Hoods. Hit it! He came from a Horror Home! Hold it! Here's a Heads up! His dad never Hugged Him that's why he still wears Huggies. He thought the Himalayas was up a Hill in the Heights of Hot & Humid Houston. How in Hell? smfH ...

He is a Horrendous Husband who is Hated by everyone, even by His Hoars because of His bad Habits. Dots get connected wrongly in His Head thats why He Hugs flags and Hopes Covid goes away. His Head is not Healthy. Holate! Holate! I Heard He Has a Huge Hole in His Head. It's like ... so Hollow, but "no one ever Heard that, nobody ever Heard that", thats why He is so Hinged on Hydroxycloroquine. This Halfwit's Healthcare plan is Heartless and Hard-hearted. He is Hard Headed, and

Harbours a Hateful and Horrendous Heart to Humanity. He is Harsh and Horrible with Hybrid Habits of a Hippo, a Hyena and a Humpback. His Horrid lack of Honor combined with the way He Hideously Humiliates the History of the U.S is so Horrible, that's why he is so Historically unpopular. I say He should be Held Hostage in a Hut near Hellville with Horrendous and Hypocritical Hopee Hicks, Harris & Hot Headed Humpty Hannity. Hollaaa … Hahahahaha

donAlphabetics

I

1

It Is what It Is. This Insane Idiot Inveigled his way Into the White House In 2016. He Is Ignorant, Inept, Ill-mannered, and Ill-informed. He Is Incompetent, Immoral, and Immature. An Intellectual deficient Imbecile. It Is what It Is. An Inveterate liar who constantly Insinuates, Instigates and calls for Investigations Into Innocent Individuals. It Is what It Is.

2

Incomprehensible, Ignorant Idiot-In-chief, Insists that his Inheritance was Insufficient. Insulting, Impossible Immigrant-hater Incapable of Informing Intelligent Immigrants why they can't Inhabit this country. His Imbecile supporters Inhale his Insurmountable lies and defends his Inexcusable Incompetence. They Insist that he is Interesting, Insightful, and Infallible Instead of Imbalanced, Irresponsible, and Irrelevant. Interrupting Institutions with his Incorrectness and his Isms.

Indeed, he Is an Intolerable Imbecile!

3

President Inept Idiot will do anything Ill advised, Impossible and Illegal to Intrude and Invade In order to cause Illness and Injury. It's been reported that he Is Ignorant on History, Ignorant on Diplomacy, Ignorant on Government

Dumbnald's Ideology is Immature, Illiterate, always Illogical and he's definitely living In an Illusion. His Ineptitude Ignored the Infected covid cases. Instead, this Impatient & Indecent Imperialist Interfered with International Imports, Inexcusably Infecting the Income and Investments of Institutions and Irritated Individuals. His Ignorance Is equal to Insanity. He thought Isis was a flavored Ice cream. So damn Immature, that's why he Inflated crowd sizes at his Inauguration. Always Insecure and Incorrect that's why Americans cannot Invest In his Insufficient Incapabilities.

He Is Infested in Inflicting Insignificant Insults with Inferno-type Ideology. We must Instantly Interfere In his Ideas Interface, and Inject some non-Important Ingredients like Indium, Iodine and Iridium In some sort of Imprudence, to avoid his Illustrative & Incomprehensive Inconsistency Indeed! Ingest that! Go on the Internet. When In the International spotlight, he Insulted National Intelligence with his Incorrect and Inexplicable, "I don't see why It would be Russia" response. What an Inappropriate Image! President Idiot and Idle Ivanca should be Imprisoned In Individual Infirmaries deep In Isolated Indiana with no Iphones & Icloud Interactions.

In an Independent Interview on ISX from Ingalls Indiana regarding his Ideas on Infrastructure, this Inexperienced, Ill-advised Imbecile was so Immature with his Imaginary Illusion, that reporter Iman Ican Immediately Imploded, then Interrupted the Interview and Instructed the Idiot that

Imprisonment will be Inevitable, due to his Impulsivity and Instabilities on such Important Issues. Infuriates Intelligent scholars with his Ill-suited and Inarticulate Idiocy, while forgetting that he Is shamefully Illustrating his Iconic Impeachment Insignia. This always Inaccurate and Inarticulate Idiot has been Impeached due to his Improper, Inadequate, Impaired, Insight and lack of Integrity.

Intolerable Inmate Ignoramus has Icky Internal Issues, that's why he was so Influential in attempts to Inject and Ingest the Impossible. Now with Increasingly, Insufferable, and Intolerable death, Injury and other Irritating Instances, this Indecent Idiot's response is no more than an Improper and Irresponsible:

"It Is what It Is".

President Inept Idiot Intimidates Immigrants with his ICE raids. So Inhuman, Incapable and Insane with his Inflaming Insults to American Indians. An Icon of Incompetence and Ignorance, who Is Immune to Intelligence. It's Incomprehensible that this Illiterate Idiot and Idle Ivanca are not yet Incarcerated. I'm done with this Irritating Idiot!

donAlphabetics

J

1

A Jealous Job killing Jerk. A Junking fool who insults and lies about everything and everyone. When he gets called out, says he was Just Joking ha! Ha! Ha! No one likes your Jokes, you Jackass! You revived the story on Joe of the morning, saying that lots of people want to know what happened to his secretary. You Jealous Jerk!! Joblessness is on the rise and more than 231 000 people dead under your watch, and your focus is on Joe (Not sleepy Joe!). You are really Jittery these days, the sleepy guy has you awake all night. Now Joy to the Reid got her own evening show and will Jazz up the night with your people Jeering at you. You are a damn joke!

2

Just so many Jokes can be made about that Junior Judgmental Jackass who thinks like Juggling Jester and acts like his Job is a Joke. Junk spills from his Jaws every time he Jabbers. His Juvenile behavior Just Jerks my mind and makes my Jewelry Jingle. We are Jaded by his constant lack of Justice and good Judgment.

Hope this Jerk does not last past January and gets Jinxed all the way to the Japanese Jungle. It would be such a Joy!

3

What a Juvenile! President Junkyard Jerk is a Jittery Jealous-of-Obama Junky who puts Americans in Jobless, Job-killing Jeopardy. This Jumbie is like a Joker on a Joyride who always gets Jammed in a Jagged Jigsaw. This orange Jailbird always Jumps in the faces of Justified Journalists with his Jargonistic Jumbling Jaw. "It's just like the Flu, Just like the Flu". On June 14th Jake from Statefarrm told him, "hey Jackass, I don't deal with Jailbirds". He always takes Jabs at Juan, Jose, Jesus, Juevo and Juanito. That's why he is clowned nightly by the Joyous, Jubilant and Jovial J's like Jake, James, Jesse, Jim, Jimmy & John, but he gets Jiggy with Jeffery Epstien, Jim Crow laws and his Judicial herpes Justices. I'm sure Jeff Sessions can't wait to see him, Jobless don Jr, and Jailbait Jared the Janitor, not wearing his Jockstrap, but instead, orange Jumpsuits, Journering to a Junky Jail deep in the Jamaican Jungle, while sipping from a Jerrican of Jello from Jackass Juliani's Joystick Jerk Juice. Jeeez.

donAlphabetics

1

Many people are saying that he has a degree in Kremlinology. Many people also say he suffers from Kwashiorkor. When he sits there's a Kerplunk sound. He thinks he has a Knockout bod. His Keratoid face is Kinda Kaka, Kook, a Know nothing Knucklehead. All he does is Kill Kill Kill Kindness. But Kama Kama Kama Kama Mamala is kinda cool!! We all know about her. She will Kick his butt.

2

This Know-it-all King of Twitter Keeps Kicking people of Knowledge. He associates with KKK lovers and tries to Keep Kids down. Does his daughter's Kitchen have Kosher food? I Know his doesn't. He's as huge as King Kong. He Kills our spirit. I want to Kick mister all the way to Korea.

Knucklehead is Kink-faced, wannabe King of KKK. Knowingly Killing Kindness of knowledgeable Kind-hearted kindred. King

donAlphabetics   35

KKK belongs in Kindergarten with other Klondike kids. Keep Kicking King in his Kaka-pants.[37]

3

President Kangaroo Karwant Knows nothing. He only has Knowledge of Krooked Kriminal activity. He's still living in a Kingsize Kindergarten Kingdom. Krackhead is still Krazy about not being in the "Kars for Kids" Kommercial. This Kook Kisses up to Kim Junk Uh, KKK Knights and Kindness with other Kremlin Kooks. This orange Knucklehead got his Keystrokes from the departed Keyboard of Kelly-Ann Konway and Killer Bryan Kill-me "The Knife." They are Killing Americans with Corona, and blaming electricians for not providing adequate Kilowatts to hospitals.

While taking a Knee in his Kitchen, he slipped on spilled Ketchup and broke his Kneecap. This was reported by Kaylee to Katelyn, Keilar and Kasparian. This Knobhead in his usual Kiddypool of Khaos, Knows that he will be Kicked out like a Kriminal in November, so during a global pandemic Krisis, he is now busy Kicking off a Kanye/Kim ticket. Is this why Kelly Ann left this White House in Krisis? He got Knocked down not Knowing that he was being Kidnapped from a Kiosk in Kentucky, a few Kilometers from where Kokabura Kofi was flying his Kite in Kettering Kommons.

While Kriminal Kyle is Killing people in Kenosha, and the McKlausky's are Menacing the Masses with their Murder Machines, Kooky Kimberly Genocide is sKreaming Krap at the Krazy Krime ridden RNC Konvention.

---

[37] Kaka (Papiamento) – Poop, stool, excrement.

K-pop Kids Killed his Krimminal family's recent rally, so he took on Kamala in a Kickboxing challenge. Kamala Kicked him like a Kickdrum and Knocked out his Kidney. Then she told him: "Sir, on January 20th, 2021, I will be the next Vice President of the United States of America". KAVAL!! ... Kamala then told him go fly a Kite in Kansas, but he Knew nothing about Kiteflying. Ai Karamba!

Kamala told him, "Sir, your Keycards are Knotted in Krime and Korruption, btw ... "Sir, can you locate Kansas City on a map?" You Konfused idiot. She then told him, "Sir, how about some Kalypso Karaoke with Kings Karessah, Krazy and Kitchener?" Then we will "jump jump" to Kris Kros and Krosfyah.

This Krook went fishing on a Kayak with Killjoy Kavanaugh in Kentucky and Kaught a Kouple Kong, Karwang and Kingfish. It was strange when Kavanaugh opened his tacklebox, he had a pair of Kneepads. Ooppss ... I don't know why he would be bringing Kneepads on a Kayak.. Did he have plans of Kneeling??? Figure this Krap out.

donAlphabetics

L

1

A Lazy, Lumpy, Lackluster Liar. Likes to Lambaste and Lament. The Laughingstock of world Leaders. He is a Leech, a Loser, and a Lunatic. Looking forward to November when this Loathsome Lizard and his Laughable Lazy Lackeys are Literally dragged out of the White House for a Livid Lampooning.

2

Leaping Lizards! Long this Lonely Lunatic Longed to Lead this Land. Lustful Loser! Likes Lots of Love from the Leaders. Look how lucky he is to have Leverage with the Locals! His Life is like a Lemon that cannot make Lemonade no matter how much Low carb sugar you give it. He Lost his Level-headedness a Long time ago. He is a Lazy Lousy Lunatic Living his Life in Lies. Preys on Lesser Leaders. Likes Leaving Lawyers Lamenting. He has Lived in Washington too long. Let's Lobby so he Loses his Location and Legacy.

3

President Liar Lowlife's Language and Listening skills gets Low results. Lou D, Laura I, Larry K & Limbaugh have Looted what's Left of his Little brain. Looney tunes has Lost his mind again. He doesn't know the Longitude & Lattitude of Louisiana or Louisville. Laura Koates said "He conflates things. "Limited words from a Lovely Lawful Law-abiding Lady. When Last we had a Laughable Leader, who is a Leach and a Liar? Oh-ho oh-ho …, Longtime! Lock him up!

When Last we had a Lousy Leader, who is a Liability and a Loser?

Oh-oh oh-ho Longtime! Lock him up! Not Liked from Laos to Luxembourg. Loudly Lambasted in Luxurious London. 45 is the Lamest, Laziest and most Lethargic President ever! Hiding behind his Lawbreaking Lawyers and only bent on his Lawless Law enforcement, when the Looting/shooting starts BS … He was Laughed at on Laconia Ave when he stopped by for his favorite Lobster & Lamb with Lentils. He had his Left foot in his right shoe. He suffers from Listening Incapabilityisis. Lincoln project Lays out his Lack of Leadership Loudly. This Lame-duck must be Laid-off and Laid to rest. He is a Less developed, Lawless, Lawbreaker who is Lackadaisical and Lagging in Love and Likes.

He doesn't Like LeBron & D Lemon, why isn't he as Loving as Gov Lamont who is so much more Laudable. RIP John Lewis: Black Lives Matter Loves you, may the good Lord bless you. This Low-rated Laughingstock is Languished with Latency. Never a Lull, Langour or Lassitude with this Lackluster Leech. He uses Loose, Loopholes to Lure and Leverage his Lawlessness with his non-Leniency.

His Logical Fallacies and Local controls are totally lame when he says, "Largest tax cut in the history of the country", our numbers are "Lower than the world", that's why Lady Liberty called him "a Leach, a Liar and a Loser" Leos and Libras find him very Loathy.

His Last-ditched Leadership effort is to send unLawful agents to maintain Lethal Law & order. He is a Low-Life Loaner, that's why he Leaks Lenghty intels to Lawless Leaders. He has no Love for Lonzo Lorenzo, Louis Farakan or Lanita Leonardo. Looks Like there's a Little Leakage when he sleeps. Who says Law markers for Law makers?

To him, anyone who is Large and Lawful is Left Leaning and Life threatening. Acts like he Loves Lincoln, but is not Liable to respect the Laws of the Land. He will Leave a Lame and Loathsome Legacy for Lifetime. His Lifelong Lawyers are all Locked in Limbo.

"Someone came up to him in Lafayette Louisiana saying: "Sir, what happened to our Livelihood? What happened to our Leadership? What happened to our Liberty? We are Lost, and tired of Losing! Because of your Litany of Lies, Please Leave", you Loaded questions Lamebrain.

Due to his Lapse in Learning and Listening, he is very Laconic in his speech or when being Lectured to. More Leaning to being Lascivious and Licentious with the Ladies. Adrian Lawrence sighs on his Lowly, Ludicrous, Limitations and Lewdness. Lord have mercy. This Lonely Loveless Lifeless Limp is not a Lady's man. President Limp Loathsome is a Lamentable Loser. Later.

donAlphabetics

M

1

Mary Mary quite contrary. What Makes your uncle blow??(fumes I mean) That book is a blockbuster gurl!! Uncle is a Miserable Malicious Monster, a Misguided Maniac and a Manipulative Mobster!! He just couldn't stop Mary. Mary say Met jell ou![38] Who in their right Mind would Move to give this Maggot a second term? Makes Me shake My head in disgust like My friend Mika in the Morning. This pathetic, Miserable Mad Man Must Move to Mar a Logo and Market Melanie as a Meaningless Model that she is. Have a Marvelous Monday Morning everyone!! And un biaha Mas[39], Merci[40] Mary!!

2

Man! How Many of us detest this Misguided, Misinformed, Moody Maniac! He is Money hungry, Malicious and May I say Menopausal. He and his Massive butt and his Many Matrimonial

---

[38] Met jell ou (French Creole) – She will kick your Ass
[39] Un biaha mas (Papiamento) – One more time
[40] Merci (French) – Thank you

40

Mistakes. A Misogynist but at the same time a Man whore. This Monster is a Mess! May I also Mention that his Micro penis should be Mashed up in a Machine? Many men would be Moved by this Marvelous Motion. He's a Moral-less Minister of Misery, Mad about his Miniscule Mittens, Menaces society with Mean-tweets of Made-up Motivations to Move his Many Maggot Muppets. Masses are motivated to remove the Malignant, Melanin Made-up Monkey from Americas Mansion back to Molehole in MaraLago.

May he Meet Many Misfortunes to Make amends for Misguided, Mean-spirited Manipulation of the MAGA Minions to Make-American-prestige-Go-Away. Move out, Mister!!

3

President Mental Madness is a very Much unstable Menace. His Mixed Messaging strategy and Mafia Mob boss Mentality causes Major Mayham and Mass Malfunctioning. He tried to Make the Mississippi run through Mara Largo but Miguel & Manuel from Major Mining & Manufacturing told him "U have to pay Mucho More Mas Money to Make it happen, U Mad Moron." They're back in Madera Mexico btw … This is how he spelt Mississippi: Me-c-c-pee. He got it Mad wrong so he Made corrections: Missy-see-p. Magwaysa. … his Miniscule Memory Murderous Maggot is always Moaping around while Manufacturing some Malicious Misery on the Masses. The Midrange frequency on his Mystery Mixer is Magically Missing. His Mangled Mouth Makes the Most Miserable Moans:

"More than ever before",

"More than we've ever seen before",

"the Most testing in the world",

"Most people don't know", which Means: he didn't know.

He knows nothing of the March on Washington,

he says "law Markers" for "law Makers". He should be kept on Mute, or Maybe Muzzled.

What type of Mad Man takes the Montreal Cog. Ass.. test and has the Mental nerve to travel from Miami to Minnesota to Maine saying: "person, woMan, Man, caMera, tv"? oh My goodness ... He Never liked Marooon 5. Mental Madness thought it was a Moslem group with Musicians from Mozambique and Morocco, Managed by Mohammed Malaka. This Madman was stunned when told that Metro North trains also travel south. "Madness! said Moron". Because he is so Mindless, he Misunderstands and Mispronounces. He Mocks and Molests people, but he Makes Miscellaneous Mistakes and Miscalculations. Orange is Messed up. He thought M.I.T was in Marlboro Meadows, Maryland.

Why does he want Mexico to pay for his Meaningless, Malevolent wall, but he keeps calling Mexicans Murderers? Why didn't his Maledict Mom have an Malodorous abortion? Who Makes Malayway[41] things like that?

This Mentally unstable Malady is the Most uninformed person ever! He Mixes up his Malaria Medication for his Migraine Meds. "Nobody ever knew the difference". Like the Massive Muller probe wasn't Malaise enough, this Manaic Merchandises Malignant Malice and Malcontent with Mishap and Mischief to McCabe and Michal Kohen.

So hear this: Dr Marcus Miles from Mankato Minnesota, Mentioned to his Maid, Melanie and his Mama, that this Merciless

---

[41] Malayway (French Creole) - Poor

Monster has a Mild to Major Mucus in his Memory. Meditate on that.. Sad to Mention, but he will be Making tracks in November.

Malkasay[42] Mercilessly Manipulates the Masses with his use of the Military. Always in a Merciless Mental, Meltdown Masquerade with his Miserable Misbehavior and Misinformation. He, with his Mini Midget size Manhood, is the Most racist Man in Merica, believe Me. Melanie got Mad when he called her Mampy, she said "Call me Mother or Mammy". This Misogynistic Monster Mentioned to Melanie, about having another kid, she asked him, "Who is the first one?"

Mika from MSNCB says he is Misdirected and Misguided. Then she Mentioned to him that Manhattan wasn't the NY state capital, he responded "Nobody knew that, nobody knew". He is totally Mixed up with the difference and similarly of Mail in/ absentee ballots. That's because his Mara largo pals has his lack of Memory, Metrics, and Matrix totally Manipulated in order to Mess up the Moral of Merica.

I hope the MAGA Moving trucks and the MEGA garbage trucks are getting ready to Move into DC to haul out all the Millionaire Mobsters. Mike by his pants the Malicious, Melanie the Mosquito, Mnuchin the Mobster, Meadows the Molester, McConnell the Misleading,

Murtaugh the Murderer, Mike Pimpeo the Majician, Manafort the Monkey, and all the other Messed up Menacing, Muddafuckers.

---

[42] Malkasay (French Creole) – Badly Bred

donAlphabetics

N

1

A Negative Numbskull who Neglected his duties. A Noisy loudmouth with a Nasty, Nauseating Attitude. Every Night he has Nice, Naughty dreams of Nancy Peletin in sexy Negligee. But she is way too much for you, you Nincompoop. A Nobody who has to be told Numerous times to wear a freaking mask. Needless to say, in November you are NAPOO[43]!!

2

Newsflash! This Narcissistic Neurologically-impaired Nutcase is a National disgrace! Naturally we can Never mention his Name. It is Necessary that this Nincompoop be Nixed from this Notable position. He is a Notorious Negro-hater. Never correct, Not Nice. His Name makes me Nauseous. Not my president! We Need a New Negro to be Named Now. For the Next Nine Nights Never Neglect to Negotiate for a New president. November will be here soon. Let Nothing and No one stop you from Naming a New President!

---

[43] Napoo (British English) – The end, dead, finished.

3

Newsflash! Newsflash!

What Nonsense was this Nagging Narcissist talking about when he mentioned Nuking hurricanes? President Name-calling Notorious Nuisance makes New enemies daily because he is Not well. He eats Nothing Nourishing or Natural, His Nutritionist feeds him Nachos, he also hates Nature. This Noisy Nosy Nag insists on being Nasty and Negative. Such a Noxious, Noisome Nitwit.

Having Neglected the News on Covid-19, with his Nightmarish Negligence, Numpty uses strategic Nonsense like News about Nasdaq, dismantling Nafta, Noose and Nascar, just Name it, so he Needlessly Nauseates the Nation with his Nonsensical Nuances. This clinical Narcissist with this Nepotism and Neurotic behavior has to be Negated to Nirvana in November.

President Nummed by Nonsense speaks in double Negatives. No collusion No Nothing, Never spoke to Nobody, Never saw No one, Didn't go Nowhere. Who speaks like this? The NY Times reports that he is Not someone who understands things, he understands Nothing and this Numbskull New Yorker is Not ok.

This Naughty, Noxious Nobody Nefariously lied by saying he took 95 North to Nevada and New Mexico. Not true! Here's another one even Nancy my Nine-year-old Niece in Nashville knew: He Never knew Nottingham England had Nukes. Oh No! Here's more, He said: "Nobody knew that I-95 runs south in North Carolina", until he found out on Nickelodeon. He Naively lied by saying he Never met, knew or heard of Nadler or Nancy. Nonsense!!! Nobody knew he has a Nicer house than Osama ... Who cares? "Numbers like No one has seen before." "I know

Nothing about her, I have Never seen her." "But Nobody likes me" ... Oh No!

Why does this Nanny go Nonstop saying?:

"Nobody ever dreamt this possible,

Nobody wanted to close the border,

I don't know the situation". But the classic was during that famous November News conference in NYC, when he asked reporter Neville News from the NJ News pool, "Why do cars travel east and west on the Northern State pkwy? Why not North?" This Nauseating Nincompoop is definitely Not Normal.

This Nettlesome Narrow-brained Neurotic Numb is Needy and he Nervously knows that Biden is his Nemesis, so this Newborn does everything Necessary to Nitpick the Nice and Noble Biden. NyceNess!

Not breaking News, but on Numerous occasions he wasn't Nice to Nurses. Nebulous Negations with health experts like this is his New Normal. He also Nastily Niggled with First Responders, calling them Non-Responders. Why does this Noodle always confuse 1918 for 1917? Are his advisors Not telling him? Or he's simply Not listening?

Back in 93, he was overheard in New York calling Nelson, Noah and Nehemiah Nasty Niggas. Always in Negation with National Newcasters, News anchors and Newspapers. He's a Non-believer. Very Noteworthy, there are no Notes on his Notepad. Nothing.

I don't know how he Navigates through Negotiations, when Numerically, he can only count up to Nine, then repeat. He was Numb when told that New York, New Jersey & New Hampshire were Northeast Neighboring States. He said: "Nobody knew that. Nobody knew". What a Nightmare! Nationally, he should be Nonrenewable in November.

This Novice always has the Notion to do something Nonsensical like inhaling Nitrogen.

At "Nukes," (a Nude stripper joint in the North Northwest), He was Nominated to be the New weed-smoker to sit in the Non-smoking section. He thought Neptune was a stripper. "Nobody knew that Neptune wasn't a stripper".

Numerous times this Newcomer tried deporting aunt Jamima's Nieces and Nephews. This Numerous-times Newlywed is busy to reopen Nightclubs,

Nail Salons and Nurseries Nationally, like he sniffed on "Nasty Novocain."

(another Nukes stripper from North Dakota). Nationwide told him: "Sir, I'm Not on your side". Because of his Naffness, he got Notified to Null his bogus Nonprofit business. Nostalgia about this Neonate's Numerous Nuances will be very Noisy, Nasty and Negative.

donAlphabetics

O

1

It is my Opinion that this Obese, Obnoxious, Outrageous Object has an Offensive rotten Orange Odor!! He uses Oppressive language Oftentimes to cause Others to Overreact and to please his Oligarchs. An Opportunist who has a young Obedient wife because he is so dam Old and thinks he is Omnipotent.

2

This Orange Overweight Obnoxious Orangutan went Overnight from being Obviously stupid to Overbearing. We shouldn't Omit to Observe that he is Overheating. His Opinions are not in Order and Obviously not Organized. The Odds are we will be Opposed to his lack Of Objectivity for a long time.

This Overly obese, Often Offended, Odorous, Obsessed, man Opines over Obama-the-Greats Oral Offerings, Obfuscates his Own Oval Office Opinions. We Ought to Oppose Opportunist Orange's Oligarchy Orders. Organize On Our Own Or Obliterate. Oh, we miss Obama!

3

There's an Offensive Odor being emitted at President Obstructive Outlaw's Oral briefings. This Odd Obstinate uses Opportunistic Offences and Outrages his Opponents with his Obstruction of Justice and Other Objectionable Obscures.

Orange's Obsession with Obama and his Overwhelming Outrageous Outbursts and Outcries clearly indicates that Obama is Out-of-this-world, Outgoing, Outstanding and Officially, much more Official. Soon to have an Omitted Omen, Oranges is Obsequious, Obscene and Obnoxious.

Tried Over & Over to Overturn Obamacare, Only to be Overruled by his Own Opposition. His Objectionable Outrage is so Offensive that he Obdurately Overwhelms everything that he Oversees and Overlooks. I definitely thinks that he is Overheating.

I don't know why at rallies in Ohio and Oregon, this Oblique Object wanted Obama's birth certificate when he Only watches Obscenity and Old Old Vanessa del Rio porno. This Oily One-sided Offender's Opinion is clearly Off the cuff. "Obamagate"! "Osama should have been captured sooner", "Obama got Outsmarted." This is Overwhelming! He is Oddly chilled Out! Where does this Obese Obtuse Object gets his Onslaughts from?

This Outcast tried Over and Over to say the word "Origins," but Oddest kept saying "Oranges, the Oranges of the investigation". He Occasionally refers to the Pentagon as the octagon. He suggested moving it to Oklahoma. He Ordinarily mistakes Iowa for Ohio.

What an Old, Oily Oaf! Ooops …

Now that this covid Outbreak has put an Obstacle in his Operations, Obstinate is Outraged, and to the mass Outcry of all, his Only Option is to Organize Obscure, Objectionable, Offenses with his Obsessiveness.

This Omnivore Oozes sweat like the Oval Office is an Oven, and he just ate Overheated Oxtails, Okra with non-Organic Oceanic Octopus with Oregano in Olive Oil, Onioned Oysters with Omega Spread in Ostrich sauce. Obviously, an Oval Orange cake with Orange juice was On the menu. He wasn't Offered hOrderves with Omelets, because he couldn't read or spell those Obviously. Ouch!!

Talking about sweating: Expect a lot of Old spice sweating in October because of its proximity to November before he goes into Oblivion.

Having been Ostracized by many world leaders, this Obsolete, non-Operable Opportunistic Ointment is trying hard to Obliterate mankind with his Occlude and Offensive Ordeal. Of course, this is not OK.

Here's an Ode to Oblong ... Old McDonald

Oppressor, e i e i O,

Blamed the Orientals for cOrona, e i e i O

He is jealous of Obama, e i e i O,

Objection here, Obstruction there,

Outbursts, Outcries everywhere

Oversight the cOrona, e i e i O.

Can you believe if Obama had done that? We shall Overcome!

donAlphabetics

P

1

This Pathetic, Phony, Petty, Perverted Prick has Put this country in Peril. With Porky Pompous Pompo by his side they should both be Prosecuted and Punished for Provoking these Protests. His Poor leadership has Put the People in a Pandemic. He loves to Pander to Partisan Politics. He thinks screaming PRESIDENTAL HARRASSMENT will stop Investigations into his Personal finances. A whiny little Pest!! Un payaso.[44] Sometimes this Pendew[45] acts like a Puta[46] for Putin!! This Pitiful Pig is like the Plague, Playing Politics and sabotaging the Post Office. He wanted his Princess Pocahontas for Vice President. Please Please stop calling the lady Pocahontas!! Please Please let's Penalize this Poisonous, Pretentious Pest at the ballot in November 2020.

---

[44] Un payaso (Papiamento) – A clown
[45] Pendew (Papiamento) – Dumbass
[46] Puta (Spanish) - Bitch

2

People, I have been Patiently waiting for P. Permit me to mention our Pussy-Grabbing President! That Power-hungry Piece of Poop!

His Personality is like that of a Porcupine. His Performance is way below Par. He Pretends that he Prays for People and for Peace. Not a Patat!![47] He is Preoccupied with his Predecessor, the President of the People. Push him out Please!!

Pissed Poor Planning and Preposterous Public Platitudes by our Predatory, Pedophile, Pompous President who Persistently Persecutes Poor People. His Posture Pushes Plenty of Peaceful Patriots to Protest Persecution from Prejudiced Policing Policies. Pussy Pawing, Poo-Poo* pants is a Prosecuted Punk, who is Prison-bound.

3

This Peacehating Prebubescent white Pig has Paralyzed the rich & Poor People during this Pandemic. He Prolonged and Procrastinated which turned it into a global Problem. President Painful Pauper, aka President Private Puppet of Putin, loves to Payback in forms of Penalty and Persecution. Just after he Preliminarily Proposed attacking K Pop culture, he Poorly Purported the Lebanon explosion because the Puke in his brain is Password Protected. (btw, the Password is Puke45is@74). This Perjured Punk is Properly Petty and Paranoid.This Pamper wearing, Petulant child with his Preliminary Pre-K mentality was Pacified by bringing fire trucks to Play with, at the People's White House. Sad! Always in a Panicked Pathetic Pandemonium. Pervert tries to Paint his Point by Poorly Persuading People, and

---

[47] Patat (French Creole) – Not a damn

Pretending that Covid is not Prevalent. Professor Pollution has a Poor grasp on Productive things.

Packman says: "He cannot Parse and analyze data", he's Definitely not a Pedagogue because he makes the dumbest Proclamations:

"Paris is no longer Paris". Called Paradise CA, "Pleasure," "If you can Protest in Person you can vote in Person", "It was a Perfect call." Who does that? Using the People's Platform to Promote his Private Properties, Posing mask-less all over the Place, Personally Proposing his Proponent Philosophy, Posting Poo all over Twitter, more Popular than Elvis Presley ... Paaleaze.

Pimple just Puts words together like a Pre-K Professional. He Probably ate all the lead from his Purple Pencil. Maybe he should have Biden continue his term as a Proxy. So much for Poetic justice ... This Patient Poorly failed his Physical because of his Pulmonary, Peripheral, Premature, Peptic, Positive-Preductive, Paroxysmal, Pneumonia Prognosis. That why he Performs like he's always on his Period. However, for his Particular Pathogen, he was treated with Percocet, Pepcide, Peppto, Peppermint, Penzzoil, Proxximol, Paxyl, Pepsi, Pidiot*, Pstupid* and Paroxetyne. (* Patent Pending) He did that Physical at a Private Practice on Prisoners Place near the Pepboyz Parking lot in Pennsylvania PA, btw ...

Americans have to Persevere while left in Personal incredulity, also having to apply self Presavation with this just imPeached Peach Pimp. His Providence does not Propose that "Pretty in Pink" Picture. This Planned Poisoned Ploy is so not Proper.

"It started in China, headed to Prague, Poland, Portugal, look what its now doing in Portland, now it's Putting me out of 1600

Pennsylvania. Why"? "People don't ask this question ... Nobody asked this question."

He thought the Panama Canal was in Pennsburg Pennsylvania. Oh no Mr President! "Oh, because it says Panama, it's in Panama? "So why is Manhattan Beach in Brooklyn?" and here's the stunner: "Why do People Park cars in their driveways and they drive on the Parkways? Nobody knew", People don't know that" …

As much as he loves Praises, he doesn't Pray and he has a Phobia to Paying his Personal or Property taxes. ProPublica and Politico Proved that! Privately, Peach uses his Power to Pay Public Porn stars however. His Pivotal Playbook is Petty Predatory violence, Jim & Poppy reported. Abby Philip and Paula Read think that the Covid Pandemonium is a Political liability and will Perpetuate into an apocalyptic Pessimism.

What a Prognosis!

Such a Pest! Always looks Pink & Puzzled, A real Phony, such a Prolific Pervert. I blame his Preveledged Parents for them Paying People to take his SAT. He brought a Pitiful ("I call it a Plague") on America while living in Plush 1600 Pennsylvania. Protesters Pleaded their Plight, People Pitifully Puked and Poomed in Pain.

Always begging for Praises, Porky Pig thinks People don't realize that he has Presided over 231K+ deaths, he Pivots between Pro-life and Pro-death. This Parasite and Proud Islamophobe is in Peril, while Personally Profiting and Prostituting the Post Office with Joy. This Pedophile has the Proclivity to Punish those who oppose him with his Performative authoritarianism and Personality disorder. Plus, Kushner's Personal Covid Plan went "Poof", but he has Promised to Pay and Promote his "Pigs for Profit."

Based on his Poor Performative Polling which he cannot Purchase, Americans are Prepared to Put him out in order to Prevent and Prohibit him from Proceeding his non-Patriotic, Putin style Performance. Potus is so Porous that this Pandemic has slipped into the Pee, Porn, Puss and Poopoo, in his Pandemonium cranium.

Amewichens, en elecsion Novembre, nou ni poo warshay Pwel misyay avec Paytay en Plat lamei.[48]

Pampers is Practically Pointless, always Polluting and Pretending. He has to be Paused and Pushed out Promptly. Potance should not Participate in the People's Peace meal because his Pediatrician will not Permit him to Pander his Pedigree. However, he is Persistent to Prove that.

President Pulsive Paranoid's handling of the PPP has Produced a Poor Performance of his Presidential Potential, and lack of Prudence and Public trust. He Promised to never drive or ride in a Prius. Like windmills, he said, "it causes Prolonged Painful cancerous Polyps". His Phases and Polarity are inverted while he Pretends they are Proper. His Perfect Plateau is being always crossed and negative, never Parallel and Positive.

Puppy's Past and Present Prenups from current and Previous Proposals and Penetrations has him acting Purely Pathetic. So, President Pungent Pimp has Published and is Promoting a Plan to Peel off a Profitable Percentage from the People's Purse. I see a Peculiar Penance and Punishment Pouring down this Preadolescence's Paternity. His Primary Policy Perspective is to cherry Pick a Percentage of voter ballot cases at Post Offices from Paris TX to Pittsburg PA. Can you believe that is his Priority?

---

[48] Amewichens, en elecsion Novembre, nou ni poo warshay Pwel misyay avec Paytay en Plat lamei (French Creole) - Americans, in the November elections, we have to rip out this guy's Pubic hairs and fart/Poom in his palms

Look how the Pest Prevented Protocol and now Prostituting the Post Office for his Personal Private Profit. Persuading People that the elections will be Plotted and Phony.

Playing with the Pledge he made to Preserve, Provide and Protect, but instead, this non-Pedagogue Prefers to Pick, Pull and Pressure People, not knowing that we have Perceived that the Pebbles, Peanuts and Profanity in his head is his biggest Personal and Presidential Problem. He is still Pissed off because Progressive canceled his Pot Production insurance Package.

This Pigsty-mentality Prick, with (should be in Penance) Pense along with Porky Pompeo, will end up in Poverty as Private Property Prisoners with their Propaganda and Profanity.

One Problem he will never have is not being in arrears at the Patchogue Public library, because Penicillin never read any books besides Porn and Playboy, but still Profiting from his Poorly-run Pink Pussycat Porno Productions. Peace my Peeps ...

donAlphabetics

---- **1** ----

This Quarantine will cause his Quadripartite ass to be hauled off to jail where he will Quench his thirst in Quicksand. He is a Quarrelsome Quack with no Qualifications and can never answer a Question put to him. This guy will have a Quick exit in January.

---- **2** ----

This man's sanity is Quite Questionable. The Quality of his work is terrible. He lacks the Qualifications to be President. He needs to stay Quiet when he can't answer Questions or Quickly Quote others who know better than him. He needs to be Quarantined indefinitely!!

Don Quixote's unique Qualities Qualify him as the Quintessential shithead clown to occupy the Quality office.

3

This Queer Quarrelsome soon-to-be Quiznos Qualified janitor is very Questionable as a U.S President. He should be Quarantined in a nonQuiet jail with visits by Quartets of well-endowed Qualified Quaterbacks, (if U know what I mean) ... This Queer and his Qanon crowd should Quickly Quit before the 4th Quarter!

I Quote "Go back to the Presidential Quaterfinals, and drink a Quart of Quality Qlorox". Queens is ashamed of you!

donAlphabetics

---- **1** ----

This Reckless, Racist, Redneck Republican is Really Rude to Rave and Rant about the Resignation of Martis. Russia pays to kill our troops and mister is silent! Yesterday this Repulsive Rotten Reptile gave a Rambling speech like a Retard! He is a Raging Rancid Rat who is Reprehensible, Repulsive and Revengeful. My Recurring dream is that the country Rejects him soon. I Recommend that in the evenings he watches the Reidout. He will be Restful, Relaxed and Really Release all the Revengeful feelings he harbors in his Rusty heart. Then he will Return to his Revolting, Rambunctious Residence in floRida to Ruminate and Rot.

---- **2** ----

Rosy-faced Rude Radical Repeatedly Ruins it for the Republicans. Really Redundant. Refuses to learn to Read or Reason effectively. Retarded Ruthless Riot inciter. He Really should Relinquish his Reins and Retire Right now. His Rationale is always Rash, his

Responses always Raw. Remember, he Rigged the election and won't admit that it wasn't Right.

This Republican leader Refuses to Renounce Racism, even after Riots Ravage urban and Rural Residences …

Racists Regard the Reality-tv Retard as Righteous, Regardless of how Repugnant his Rhetoric is. He is a Putin Rag-doll who Refuses to Recognize that Russia is Really Responsible for his Reign. His Remedial, Rambling, Reading Rarely Reflects Reality and Regardless of Response or Re-edits, it will remain on Record for Research.

Remove him to Repair the Ruins.

3

Roger Roger!

This Rotten Revenge-seeking, Republican Rat is such a Radical, Racist Rogue! This Rebellious, Rasclat, Raggamuffin is always in a Rage. President Rascal Restless Riot-seeking is continuously on a Rampant Rant.

He has Ramshackled the economy into a Rocky Road like he wants to Return to a Recession, so his Revolving door of morons, Rejects and Redundants won't be Restricted to Roam and Rape at free Range.

There is no Room for his Reactionary Recipe and total lack of Responsibility. His Replacement will be a Rebarbative Reaction of his Rude Reluctance to Respect and be Reasonable. His Refusal to Read and Respect Real Recommendations and Research is Remorsefully Repulsive and Rattling. Never Relaxed or Restful.

Refuses to Retract a Regrettable Reporting. Like a Rare Rash, Rampant Radical Rage and Racism Ravages this Revengeful Retard! Why would this orange oRangutan Roll back Remarkable, Renowned environmental and clean water Regulations?

For some Rare Reason, he gets Riled up with Raoul Ramirez, Rudy Rohas, Roberto Rodriguez and Romeo Ricardo. He thinks they are Rapists from Ranas y Refugio, in Rural Mexico. He lied saying that it was Reported by RNN Regional. He also hates Rastafarians like Ras Radical from Richmond Ridge, Rhode Island, and Ras Rakattack from Reddington Region. "They don't Raise the Red flag".

Such a Rebuked, Repulsive, Runaway, acting like Radical Roosevelt from Rozo. He's in his Radiant Rapture when Roaming with Rats like Rogger Stone, Ruthless Rudy Julianii and Reckless Rosh Limbaugh the Retarded Russian. He has Ravaged and Rampaged civilization and American democracy. He Reads like Reading wasn't Recommended for him that's why he Repeatedly wanted everyone to Read the transcripts. He thought Route 66 takes you to Route 67. When corrected, he said "nobody knew that, nobody knew".

For no Reason, he Ridicules Reggae and Relaxed RnB during Romance. He Rolls with Rap, Ragtime and Rock & Roll during his Risky Russian Roulette Relationship. What a Relentless Roughneck!

Always looking like he ate some Rare Roasted Rabid Racoon from a Rural Russian Restaurant. His winning Ratio in being Reelected is like Rowing down a a Rocky River during a Rainstorm. His Reluctance and de-Railing Response to Covid has Repressed America's Revenue. He should stop being Resistant and Retreat to his Restless Resort. Now this Repulsive Rotton Rabid Rogue is Recommending his Ratface on Rushmore among the Real

Radiant Respectables. Not a fan of Reading or Religion, but Radio and tv Ratings brings Relief to this Rashole. Retard knows nothing about the Republic, did no Research on voting Registration in any Region, but his Resolution is to Rampage Rumors and Resources in order to Rule the election Race. Reddit Reported that he says Ridiculous things, and he doesn't Remember what he says. Rachel says "he makes stuff up", like Raking floors in Sweden. ROF says he "doesn't understand Roe V Wade". His Rectifier needs to be Rectified. Because of his Reprehensible Repeated lies, he's always being Rejected and Ridiculed. We need Repellant to eradicate this Repugnant Republican.

Reprehensibly Refuses and Rejects the Right and Rational Rule of Law with his Rebellious Reckless Refutation. This Repetitive Repulsive Racist has a Rotten non-Remorseful Reputation. Always Recoiling and Retaliating after being

Reprimanded for his non-Respectful Repugnance.

This Ringleader's Ruthless Role has to be Regretfully Rebuked as he Requests a Reason to be Reinstated. His Covid Recovery Report has to be Reviewed, and in Reality, his Record has to be Refuted. Here he is Reigniting a trade war with Rwanda, Romania, Russia and Rest of the world, Reaffirming that: "I have the Right to", I'm the Rogue President". This Rabbit Ranks worst in world leaders. When Ratface dies, his tombstone on his Rural Real estate will Read RIP, but it will Ritualize: "Rot in Peace". Good Riddance, you Rotten Rat! No Room for you in the Rotunda. Election day will make you Redundant for Rest of your life.

Roll de Riddim!!!

donAlphabetics

S

1

So Sad, he has that Same Sarcastic Savage Smile, well he can't Smile, he Smirks. A Selfish Senile Soul. Does he have a Soul? Is he Successful? Is he Smart? Is he Spiritual? Is he Sexy? Is he Sympathetic? No no no!! So, he is a Senile, Special-educated, Sadistic, Screwball.

The Sanctimonious Salop[49] was forced by his Special Services to Seek Safety in the Secret underground Safe, so that Society would not see the Smelly, Shit Stained pants from the Scaredy-cat. You Should have Studied harder. Not pay your Buddy to take your SAT test for you. Fool, learn to Speak Softly and carry a Strong Stick. Said he would drain the Swamp! Now the Swamp has become a Clogged Sewer, Seeping it's Slimy Stinkipoo all over the Sun!! You Spit on the Constitution by pardoning your Slimy, Sinister, Sludge-buddy Stones.

He thinks the Supreme Court is there to protect him! They Suddenly See him for the Senseless Sleaseball that he is.

---
[49] Salop (Frehcn Creole) - Slut

Someone please Slap the Shit out of him so we can Soon Start Singing Save us, Save us maker of the world!!

2

So! That Slimy Shameless Snake Seems to Somehow Say that Since he was Sworn in, Systems have been running Smoothly. Such Statements are Stupid, Selfish and Senseless. He is a Sad Skank who Sleeps with every Slut that he can get his Sticky hands on. He Stinks of Sewer! Students and Seniors cannot be Saved by this Savage. Shame! By September, people Should be Smart enough to See Straight and not Select this Stupid man to Stay in the Same Spot that he Seems to enjoy. Shoo, Salop![50] He is a Senile, Special-educated, Sadistic, Screwball.

The Sanctimonious was forced by his Special Services to Seek Safety in Secret underground Safe So that Society could not See the Smelly, Shit- Stained pants from the Scaredy-cat. Speaking of Special ... Sons and Son-in-law Should Seek Some Soul Searching, along with Scalpel-face Sister. They Specialize in Speaking on Subjects in which they have no Sound Support or Specialty. Segue back to - the Socially-inept, Second grader thinks Shouting Shows Strength - Stupid-ass, you should have Stayed in School to learn to Speak Softly and carry a Strong Stick. Stupid Says that he Studies Scriptures, but Shows with his Small, Slimy hands that has never seen a Sentence or pSalm in that Sacred book.

Someone please Slap the Shit out of him, so we can Start Singing Songs of Solomon.

---

[50] Salop (French Creole) - Slut

3

How Sad, how Shameful! www.SatanSupporters.com Says that Satan was Shocked, Stunned and Surprised when he Saw Some of the Serious Shit that this Super Shoplifter has Solicited and Strongly Supported. Satan Said: "Sir, it's no longer a Secret, you are Sick and you Seroiusly Suck".

This Staten Island Snake oil Salesman needs to get back on the Small School bus, then go home to watch Sesame Street. Seriously!! He only went to School on Sundays in the Summer, but Slept through it all. Now Biden is the one he's calling Sleepy Joe because he's so Scared. What a Shithead! For all the Strange and confusing Spit balling which comes off the Small crevice in this Scoundrel's head, (aka his Speech Source) he should Surely

a) Wear a Smart mask,
b) Stop talking. Just Shut da f*#k up!

His Sunday Best Speech Sounds Shitty, like the Smell of Spoiled Sardines in the Summer. Shamefully, his Syntax makes no Sense. From the Standpoint of Stupidity, this Scumbag Supercedes. That's why Statefarm told him, "Sir like a bad neighbor, your Surroundings Smell like Shit!". Every Sunday Spongebob Sipps a Special Sample of his Stupid Sauce, from his Salty Sautéed failed T Steaks, then he and Steve Mnuechin Sew Sweet seeds from the S&P and the Stock Market having a Sunny day. Who cares? All your Superior Scams System and your Strategic nonsense is taking the country down a Slippery Slope, you Snakes! From the Standpoint of Smartness, this unStable genius is a Sickening Skunk. He is not Someone who understands Simple things but Shouts out Strange Sounds that he is a Smart cookie. "I don't Stand by anything". "Space Force", Space Force"! "It Should have been Stopped in China". The Soviet invasion was justified. "From the Standpoint of water, it's very wet hurricane!" WTF??Always Speaking in Superlatives: "The Saddest day for the Stockmarket, the Strongest military, the Safest bunker in DC. Then Silly Switches to the Shameful Statements like: "Why do cars travel east and west on the Southern State pkwy? Why not South? Makes no Sense. Nobody knew that!"

The Stupidity in his Seized Scrambled eggs has him Speaking in tongues. Shit like unproven "Surveillance and Spies in my campaign", "raking forests in Sweden", "kids only have Sniffles", "Stormy Daniels was the Sweetest Slut but I never knew her, I never Slept with her", "the virus is under control in the Sunshine and Southern States". Such Sickness! This Spalpeen thought that Social Distancing was a Swedish online Stripper and the Stimulus package was a Sexual Slang. "Really? The Stimulus package is not Something Sexual? Nobody knew that".

For some Special reason, he doesn't See eye to eye with Sergio Salvatore, Sanchez Salazar, and Santino Sabina. Stony-hearted Swine Says they are part of the Secret Savage State Sponsored terror Squad. This SOB echoes Tom Cotton's "Slavery was a necessary evil" myth, aJones "Sandy hook conspiracy", and other Similar Stinkers from Seducee, Shannity and jKush with his Stockpiles, Stockpiles, Stockpiles Sick, Sad Shameful Song. That's why when he Speaks Roseta Stone be like whaaaat? jSwan thought he was interviewing Someone Sick with both Scurvy and Syphilis. Seriously lacking Sustainable Smarts to barely Survive. Did U See the Surprise Stare on jSwan's face?

The Stigma of this Shameless Skank's Stomach-churning Sadness is nightly Sung and Satirized by Seth & Steven. During a Sad and Severe pandemic, President Stifle & Suffer makes Silly disinfectant Suggestions, then Says he was just being Sarcastic. Spoiled Statements like he didn't know that Southwest airlines fly to the north-east States. "Woww, Nobody knew that."

America, we are Stronger and Smarter than that. We Surely have to Sweep this Stained Swine out before he Suggests Subletting the White House, like how he wanted to Sell Puerto Rico, to Snakes and Sexist like Steves Bannwagon, Miler and Scavino.

Sicko Said that he went to Stop & Shop but be didn't stop, and he didn't shop. He Simply kept walking and Surveying Short Skirts. Then Sandra, the Senior Salesclerk came up to him Saying, "Sir, you have to Stop it, and Shop, hence the name, Stop & Shop". Salop responded: "Oh Sweetness, why didn't Someone Say So earlier? I Should have been Shorter, So I could See more of the Sweet Specific Samples."

From the Standpoint of national Security, this Shituation is Seriously Shitty and lacks Specificity. During the Shameless Shock of the Pandemic, Skunk is Spending time golfing, Smiley Satan is forcing States to beg for Covid Supplies like we are Sorry Supplicants. But that's fine my dawg, it's all good. The Strict and Solemn SDNY will Slap your Sorry ass hard for all the Stolen taxes you Siphoned from NYS and you will be Sprayed in Salt and Shame. I only hope you can Swim because there will be So much Skunky Seamen up to your Shoulder in your Slippery Stony cell, your Scarpered Self will be Struggling to Stand Straight. Studs like Strong Sal and Sugarcane Salsa, aka the Sweetest Scorpion, will Satisfy you with their Special Saccharine Syrup. Your Slithered Self will be So Sick that you'll Secrete all the Shit from your Stomach, and all your current Sweet Samaritans will be part of this Savage Salvo. Shove off! You Sneaky Stinky Slut!!

donAlphabetics

1

This Two-faced Toddler Takes Too much valuable Time on Twitter, instead of Taking charge. He Turned the Troops on and Teargassed innocent citizens. A Terrible Two-faced Tyrant. A very Troubled man who Talks like a Two-year-old. The Truth is his enemy. He Committed Treason by Taking intelligence findings from our enemies instead of allies. His Taxes are still under audit. How much Time does it Take to Tally someone's income and expenses? Let's Talk about That!! It's only a matter of Time when he will be Taken out of The people's house and Tossed in The Trenches with his Russian Translator.

2

Today I want To Tell you guys about That Terrible Tyrant in the country's Top position.

A Toxic terrorist who Tells people whatever is on his Tiny mind regardless of whether or not it is True or Touches reality. To him, The presidency is about Talking Too much and Telling Tales. He

Tasted power on the Apprentice and now he wants to Treat people like we are his Temporary employees. He has The Temperament of a Troubled Teenager. Time To go, Tonneh miseh!![51]

3

This Tragic Top-heavy Tyrant is always in a Toxic Tralala. While being extremely Tangled and Trashy, Tangerine Titan is actually Trafficking Terror, and he is Terribly leading America into Temptation and Transgression. Why does This Thorny Thief always Trouble, Touture and Torment people with his Temper Tantrum? Thug is so Thoughtless with his Thumbs-down Totalitarian Toughness, That Americans are Terrified by the way They are Trampled and Trumpled on like Toentoen.[52] Everything This Terrorist Touches Turns into Tragedy. I'm hoping the Titan Trailers and Terrific Trash Trucks are ready To Take out This Temporary "President Trashy" and his Thugs from the White House because he's been Tragic with covid Testing, Terrible with Truth & science, he Tarnished Tammy D, Turnovers guilty verdicts, committed Too many Tax frauds and Treason, Turmoil and Tension with Trade, Threats of Terror against Toppling statues of Tyranny, and he's also a Thief who has TipToed and Thieved The nation's Treasure, while causing Total Tragedy and Trauma with his Thoughtless Tweets. Tweeter in Chief is Tripping. Takeaway The phone he uses to Tantalize and Terrorize from his Tiny Thumbs. Take him off Texting & Twitter, Take him off The WH, put him in Total confinement. This Traitor is Toxic with his Tricks and Treachery. His Toilet Trainer, Teacher Tamron Tease, (a Taurus) born in Tazewell, Tennessee but moved To Three Way, TN, was Teaching him To use a Toothbrush and a Toothpick, but Two-faced Twitch used The Toothpick on his Twisted Tongue

---

[51] Tonneh miseh (French Creole) - Dammit

[52] Toentoen (French Creole) – Pound food

instead. That's why he still Talks so much Trash. So, This Tenuous Tapeworm had To be put on Timeout and have him repeat: person, woman, man, camera, Tv, person, woman, man, camera, Tv, Till The Troublesome Toddler fell asleep. Then he Told Tonya his Therapist, That Throughout his life he Thought TLC meant, Trump loves corruption. When corrected by Tonya, he didn't Thank her but he said "nobody knew That, nobody knew".

We are Tired of This Toilet mouth Trash Talker who TYT describes as "not someone who understands Things, even when reading a Teleprompter". Besides being Tone deaf, did U miss Tim Apple? Tremendously wet? Two Corinthians? While being Thanked by Tactless Tucker C for his Tainted Toughness, Traitor is nightly Teased by Tasteful and Talented Trevor N because of his Torment and Tumultuous behavior. This Truant has Transformed The nation into Tension and Turbulence The way Topsy-Turvy Tags To make his point. Teacher Tamron from Tazewell/Three Way should put him back on Timeout.

This Tarnished Thief needs To be Tamed and Tased because people are Tired. America is Tense because of Dumbnald's Tacky Tragic Toujours[53] Taunting and Teasing with his Tedious Tiny-Thumbed Tweets. This Traitor needs To be Tanked and Toppled down a Treacherous Terrain. Whenever This Truant has To count past Ten, he Takes his Tiny shoes off. This Totalitarian is Totally Testy. Always Tense and Thin skinned, acting like he's Trapped in a Thorny Trepidant. In Three years of Tameless leadership, This Tenacious Twig has Tried and Tested the Tools and Templates of Tenuous Torture.

The world is Totally Threatened. Tajikistan, Tantan, Tanzania, Tete Morne, Thailand, Thibaud, Togo, Tonga, Tortola, Toucari,

---

[53] Toujours (French Creole) - Always

donAlphabetics

Tootoopal, Toolooloo, Trinidad & Tobago, Trafalger, Tunisia, Turkey, Toute monde[54] . Today, Tonight, Tomorrow, Tuesday, Thursday nou nee poo Toil avec Twavai pour Tiway Trump[55]. Tank and Tumble this Torpid Trollope!

---

[54] Toute monde (French Creole) - Everybody
[55] Nou nee poo Toil avec Twavai pour Tiway Trump. (French Creole) - We have To Toil and work To Take out Trump

donAlphabetics

U

1

The Unmasking of the Guy …

It was Unlikely that he would be elected in 2016. Yet, in spite of his Uncouth mouth, Unlawful behavior, Unproven accusations … he won!! He was Unloved in NYC, Unwelcome in the fancy Manhattan clubs and Unwanted by the bourgeois of Jamaica Queens. It was Upsetting to him that folks felt he was Unworthy to be in their presence. It's Unbelievable that he felt so Unwelcome and Unloved that he decided to run for office!! Undermined his own reputation and Unmasked himself.

Awo tur su keshi a sali!![56] He was Unwelcome in all circles. This is one angry dude! What Upset him the most was when a black man became President before him that was just Unacceptable!! Unimaginable! Unthinkable!! So, he decided to Undermine Obama's presidency by claiming Obama was born in Uganda!! Or Kenya. Or Whichever!! No Dummy Donnie, Obama is Unmistakably American!

---
[56] Awo tur keshi a Sali (Papiamento) – Now all the cheese have come out

2

Ugh!! That Ugly Unintelligent Ugly certainly does not represent a Unicorn (which symbolizes purity). Uneducated, Unkempt, Unstable, Unable to Understand the Utterances of educated people. He gives in to his Urges even if they are Unlawful. It is Unlikely that things will improve Unless we vote him out. Until then, we can hope that he has an Urgent Untimely death. Ultimately, he will get out of the White House and our Ulcers will begin to Undo themselves. Ugh!!!

3

Uugh! It's raining Unrest and Unproductivity in DC. Get an Umbarella ella ella, ay ay ay! Who the hell holds a bible Upside down? What an Unpopular Unqualified Useless Underbrain! This Ugly Ulcer is Unlikely to Understand the Unnecessary Unpleasantness making everyone Unsafe.

U see, President Unrestrained Unrestricted (President UU for short) is so Unpredictable, Unreasonable and Untrue, that he is Unsuccessful and Unsure at Uniting the Universe.

His Unsatisfactory and Unruly behavior proves that he is Unskilled, Uninformed and very Unlawful. It's so Unfortunate to have this Unhappy, Unscrupulous and Unhealthy Unicorn Undoing everything that Ultra, Ultimate Obama Unselfishly Utilized. Because this Unfit-for-office Understands nothing, this Unsympathetic Underdog now has Unheard of Unemployment #s due to his Unacceptable and Unclear Understanding of the United States. As Unpopular as the Unibomber, he Used to attend the UUUU. University of Unbelievable Uncharitable and Unrest. Understudy of Unmerciful, Uncaring and Unfeeling. Unclear whether he graduated because of his Unsavory, Underlying conditions such as: he is Unpredictable, Uncompromising and he Understands nothing.

This Utterly, Uncapable Unforgiving, Unscrupulous Uproar has been proven to be Unfit to Uplift the USA. Under this Unsavory (lack of) leadership, USA has Unsightly and Unspeakably been downgraded to USU.

United States of Uproar / United States of Upsetting. He is not Useful in Undertaking the Upbeat and the Upswing of Uncle Sam. Whenever he Unzips his mouth, (like his Unclear Ultraviolet bullshit) it's always an Unheard of, Unsatisfactory Unmasked Uproar. He Upsets the UK, the UN, UAE, Uganda, Uruguay, even Uzbekistan. Watching and listening to this Uuugh is like … is like … Unsanitarilly wetting your Underwear for the Umpteenth time.

I'm not Up with this Unethical Unwanted and Unseen behavior with soooo many Unresolved, Unheard of investigations. So damn Unconstitutional! Until the elections, it will be an Untold-of Unfortunate and Unfriendly Uphill Undertaking. Someone should Uncomfortably cut the Umblical from this Unborn Un American … so lucky I won't apply my Useful time to Unleash and Unload his Ukraine, "perfect call" bullshit on this Uneducated soon-to-be Unemployed Uncouth Undesirable. FU President Ugly with your Undersized hands! U damm, Unpleasant, Unhinged, Unfit to lead, soon-to-be un welfare Unsatisfactory compost heap!!

donAlphabetics

V

1

A Vile and Vindictive Viper, with a Very Vicious heart. Vibrates Venom with every word he speaks. This Virus has Vomited on his election Victory Parade. A Vagabond who is Vengeful and always plays the Victim. Dangerously rushing for a Vaccine within 3 months. Let's hope he takes a lifelong Vacation or just Vanishes in January 2021.

2

Verily, Verily, I say unto you: that Viper will Vanish from his Vocation Very, Very soon. His Vulgar behavior will not be tolerated. So Voracious for power but he takes mini Vacations. He is Vile. Vayaying[57] everybody's business. His Volatile story always has a different Version from everyone else. Insults Veterans. So Vindictive, people are scared of Voicing their feelings. Didn't Validate the information the CDC gave him so the Virus caught us unprepared.

---
[57] Vayaying (French Creole) – Watching closely

As his Views are Validated by those who choose to remain Vacant from their ideals, the Vagabond assumes Victory for his Vengeful Vicious attacks on the Voiceless. This Vermil is Vlad's puppet and is Void of Valor. Every Veteran of the Vietnam era who has served with distinction, Voices opposition to this Vagrant. He is Vehemently opposed to the investment in Ventilators for covid Victims and now Views the intubation of human Values as a Victory.

It is apparent that his Values have been Vacuumed out of his now Vacant brain and all that's left is Venomous Views. Verifiably insane and incompetent. I encourage dog to visit his Veterinarian to get a Vaccine for his Very racist Views.

3

This Vain Venomous Vagabond is such a Vicious Vulture. Orange is always Vulgar, forever Vex and Very Vehmin[58] with his Violent Vocabulary. This Vampire is quick to Vandalize the deal, becomes petty and fragile like he's been Vitrified, then plays the Very Victim like he did to Verified Veteran Vindman.

Americans must View and Verify his Varied taxes, then Vow to Veto and Validate its content. He should not be Vindicated. His Velcro/Vulcanize-type Vulgarity also causes him not to be Venerated. He Vayays[59] and Victimizes people with his Variegated Vomit.

He is always Venturing out from Virginia to Vermont on golfing Vacations. He wanted to have only Virginian Virgins as his caddies, but because of the corona Virus, he was advised to do it Virtually. He was Very pissed off. He claims that he doesn't drink liquor,

---

[58] Vehmin (French Creole) - Nasty
[59] Vayays (French Creole) - Peep

but some Vladimir Vodka would surely Vanish the Volcanoes in his head, then Ventilate its Volume of Violence and Vitriolic Vulgarity. Because of his Vehmin Vocabulary, Victor Velazquez from Venezuela living in Vermont, called this Ventriloquist a Vulture and "The Village Idiot". He said President Vulture Vomit muddled Val Demmings for Demie LoVato. Who does that? Now, with no Verification and Validation, he Vocally claims that Vann Jones was born in Vietnam. Who Visualizes and

Vocalizes this Vomit? Very sick man of no Virtue, that's why he's hated by all Virgos, and Very unwelcome at the Vatican.

Before this no Value Violator Vanishes and Vaporizes the USA, this Vaywa[60] needs to Visit his Veterinarian and get a coVid Vaccination with some Vampire Vermin in his Violent Veins, then have his Vomitous Version Vacated.

That Vieux Vash[61] always acts in a Vulturelike manner. The Vibrations he Vamps from his Voice is Vile and Volcanic. Its Vociferation is always Vulnerable to Vomit some Virus-type Verbiage. Viva Victory! That's the Verdict! VOILA! USE YOUR VOICE! VOTE THIS VILLAIN OUT!

---

[60] Vaywa (French Creole) - Good for nothing
[61] Vieux Vash (French Creole) - Old despicable

donAlphabetics

---- 1 ----

What a Wasted Womanizer! Woof!! Woof!! We can do Way better than this Woefully Whining Wuss in the White House. He is Wacky and Wild and Wishes he could Woo all Whores to his Wide, Wide bed. We all Wish he Would Wander into the Wilderness never to be seen again. He is a Wacky Wacko and a Weak Wimp! A worthless Whiner and We can't Wait to tell him WTF WTF WTF IN NOVEMBER.

---- 2 ----

Woye![62]

That Weasel just Won't leave Women alone! I hope the fact that his Wife not staying in Washington With him doesn't cause him treat the White House as his personal Whore house.

Whenever he Wants to Work his Wimpy brain he Wonders What educated people are doing and he starts to Whine. While says he

---

[62] Woye (French Creole) – A cry of distress

78

doesn't drink Wine, Why does he constantly act like he is drunk? And not only on Wednesdays either.

The Womanizer Who claims to grab Women by their Women-parts really thinks he can Woo Women into sleeping With him with his Wee Weiner.

When he thought his Woes Were over, White police began Wounding and Wiping out black people and now the War is on. Wimpy-ass President! Male Whore! Go Wash your Whale-sized ass!

What the heck you Want With us??

Wow!!! What a Wonderful World it Would be With Witty Whispers of a Worldy Wise-man.

We want: Wealth, We need: Words of Wisdom. What We got: Whinny Whimpers from a Weighty Wonderer, Wroth With Wrong Way Warnings.

Dumbnald and his Wandering Wiz-kids Want a White world, for the Wealthy. We Wish for the Welfare of the World that Would Welcome Women of Wisdom to Work Without Wrath and Workplace harassment.

What a Wicked Wonker.

When Will We Wage War on his Wicked Ways and Wash away his Wet-stain?

3

"When they go low, I go lower. When they go high, I stay low". This Woeful Wierd Womanizer is always Wrong. He is by far the

Worst and Wackiest in Washington. What a Warlike Waste Who Was Warned about the Wicked Pandemic, but the Worthless, Wretched, Whoreass, Whorebitch Wrestled With intel, Wrecked and Worsened the sHituation with his Washed-out Wrath, and Worried and Wounded the World like a Wierd Weed smoker.

Like a Woebegone Wornout Worm, this Wrinkled Wierdo makes America Weep & Weary With his Wildness, While Wailing some Waterdown Wimpy Wayayai[63], like Warning African Americans, "What the hell you have to lose?" What about a Worse one? Wiretapping the Wierdo's campaign! Or the 1967 Walter Headley phrase.

He spends his Weeknights doing nothing Worthwhile, and is always on the Wrong Wavelength on a Wholesale level. This Wishy Washy Who Wasted Wiery Weeks upon Weeks Wagging his tail like he had no WiFi, While blaming Wuhan. Now he's on every Website, because he Wants to be re-elected. What a Wizzy Whimp!

From the standpoint of Water, Which he cannot hold a glass of, this storm is very Wet! What? Apparently, he never got Stormy Wet.

WTF? He doesn't read the Wall street journal because he claims it has too many Words and he already has the best Words. While recently "Wishing her Well", he Wailed out something like, "We are lower than the World". WWWHAAAT?? are you saying? Why did we have a civil War? What are you talking about?

Woyooo Woyooo[64]

---

[63] Wayayai (French Creole) - Scream
[64] Woyooo Woyooo (French Creole) - Scream

This Whoremonger went on a Widespread Warfare to Wrong-do a Whistle-blower for doing his job. Then he Withdraws Welfare from Whoever he chooses if he is not Worshipped. Definetely not a Workaholic.

This White BIACH Wears me out, always Wedging a Worldwide War With himself, Wrongly telling America that he is Winning. Winning What?

Woyoyoi Wayayai[65] WTF? He Wants people to go back to Work but he never Works. This Wrongdoer's Workstation should be a Wheelchair begging in a Whorehouse near the Wastebasket. He said someone came up to him and said: "Sir, Work, like Windmills causes cancer". I think he's Wired for 110 but is supposed to Work on 220. That's why this Weird Whimp always blows up. Maybe he should be reWired and take away his Wireless. Wolf said, "This is the Worst thing that happened to the World. The White House Institution is Woefully Winging it". Whimp Wanted to build a Best White Western West of Western Westchester, near the Western Pork supermarket, but got pissed off when he Was told that black people live in White Plains. He said, "Nobody knew that, nobody knew", So he decided to build it in Wuhan after the Washdown. Why Would you do that? Well Well Well, What a Wierd, Wasteful, Whiny one Who understands nothing.

---

[65] Woyoyoi Wayayai (French Creole) Screams

donAlphabetics

1

Without knowing, he got a Xenograft down there. I think his Xothermatic procedure was done unknowingly to him. Maybe Pence knows about it because his head is way up that dark hole. The other part is Deric, and he is the other son that has the same issue. A Xerox copy of a fXXXed up family. Sayonara in November. Xmas will be like a major jump up in the streets like a carnival! De Blasio or Cuomo will declare a National Street Party so we can dance on 5th Avenue.

2

All I can say is that Dumbnald is eXtremely eXasperating . And sometimes I feel that he knows eXactly what he is doing. His doctor should do an X-ray of his brain to eXplain why he likes so much X-rated conversations. He always has an excuse for his actions. They are always so far from being eXcellent. He shouldn't be eXcused for his behavior. In fact he and his family eXcept the younger children should be eXecuted. After listening to this Xenophobic, I had to seek Medical eXamination. Doctor took X-rays of my brain and found that I had suffered damage from seeing his anoreXic wife doing XXX-rated movies and prescribed Xanax for my stress. The tries to X-out all of Obama's policies while his wife is not so secretly Xeroxing Michelle's speeches. If we want to return to Xanadu ... on November the 3rd, XX out of office so that we can have a happy Xmas.

3

This Xenophobe needs a complete Xray. Not with an Xray machine, but with a Xylometer. His X wives must be happy that this Xrated shithead is so unpopular. Putin played him like a Xylophone, and this is no hoaX. X marks the spot where he was played. He should have used his HydroXycloroquine and Xylenol on his dumbass and end up in Xerostomia. Xavier Xeno & Xander should Xerox BLM and Malcom X all over the damm White House. Send that orange Xenoblast into Xylogy.

donAlphabetics

---- **1** ----

Yadi Yadi Yadda!! Whenever Yamishe challenges him he calls her a nasty reporter. He hates her because she is not a Yes girl and knows her stuff.

This Yucky looking Yankee with a Yeast filled face loves to be surrounded by youthful females and behaves like a Yazuka in their presence. With Yak-like hair, he tries to make his short comings Yours.

---- **2** ----

Yow! You see that Yellow (orange). Yankee in Y'all's White House? You need to Yank him out by the end of this Year. Yes, he definitely has a defective Y-chromosome. His brain belongs in a Yard sale. When he Yelps, all I hear is Yadda, Yadda, Yadda. He and his Yacht club friends need to go to the YMCA every Yom Kippur.

He is constantly Yelling and Yabbering. He is like a damn Yellow fever mosquito in my head - or like a barking Yorkshire terrier. Yap, Yap, Yap. All Year long! Makes my head spin like a Yo-Yo. The man is a nuisance like a freaking Yeast infection. He steals whatever Youth I have left. I have to go on YouTube to find ways to deal with him. Come end of Year I want to be singing Yeah, Yeah, Yeah when he's gone.

3

President Yeast infection is such a damn Yucky Yankee, who is madly hated by the Young and old. He dislikes Yams, Yuka & Yemas. He thinks they come from Yemen, and Yemen is in Yelapa, Mexico. What a Yoya customer! He Yells, lies and steals daily. If the day ends in Y, Yes, he steals anything from Yarns to Yoyos. When told that Yellowstone national park is actually in three states, he's like: "Yaw! That's the biggest democratic hoax. Nobody knew that. Now the democrats are going to say that the YosemYte is just over Yonder in three states also." He kept Yelling, "Yaw, nobody knew that, nobody knew that Yaw."

Yesterday he went to a strip joint at the Yukon Yacht club and ran into Yasmin and Yolanda. He didn't like the Yolk & Yucky remarks, so he got pissed off, Yelled, and YapYapped them on Yelp. Not Youthful looking at all. Looks more like spoilt Yugoslavian Yogurt. This Yellowed, always Yapping, never Yielding, Youth hating, very Yolklish Yawner thought that Yogi Berra and Yogi Bear was the same person. Damn! This idiot needs some Yogi Bhajan spiritual teachings. Yucky said he saw it on YouTube. Yes indeed. If the day ends in Y, Yes, Yeasty is Yapping lies.

donAlphabetics

Z

1

He is definitely not a Zaddikim.[66] With his expensive suits, his behind looks like a Zabuton[67] or Zafu. Is it true he eats Zabaglione[68] for breakfast? The hair looks a bit different recently. Combed in a Zig Zag fashion. This quarantine has made Zoom very popular.

I wonder if he knows how to use it. He is the twitter king with Zero chance to make a comeback. Like the Zookeeper who got locked in the cage by the fox, hope he goes to Zocalo, Mexico for a Zafa![69] So, let's say Zip Zap Zaboka!![70]

---

[66] Zaddikim (Hebrew) – A person of outstanding virtue and piety
[67] Zabuton (Japanese) – A Japanese cushion for sitting on the floor
[68] Zabaglione (Italian) – Italian dessert
[69] Zafa (Spanish) – A cleansing ritual
[70] Zaboka (French Creole) - Avocado

2

Zealously campaigned to win the election, only for us to find out that he is acting like a Zany whenever he has to speak publicly. He is a malformed Zygote. His body should be flattened with a Zamboni and shipped to Zambia for them to have a field day with him.

The Zodiac signs probably identify him as a Zombie. His brain should be Zapped and Zig- Zagged all the way to Zaire. I have Zero confidence in that Zebra.

3

1600 BLM Ave is a damn Zoo. This Zulu Zombie who always walks in a ZigZag, can never Zip his lip. Always in some vieux Zaffaire[71] Zapping Zeroes. He knows Zero about Zoology and he's so dumb that he doesn't have a Zodiac sign. He claims, while in Zurich, a very Zaftig Zephyr Zamore originally from Zephyrhills FL, came up to him saying: "Sir, like Zima, Zucotto and Zucchini, which you never eat, you don't need a Zodiac sign". So he was listening to a song by Zeppelin on WZZZ called Ziploc your Zipper. "Is this song about me? If it is, It doesn't take me to Zion, It doesn't takes me to my Zenith". "It must be all about me".

Now this Zany liar claims that his bone spurs was due to high Zinc and Zymolytic calcium issues. Always making up some ZangZang bullshit! While watching a live concert with Zedd, ZZ Top and Zwarte from Zimbabwe, this Zombie got pissed off. "Look at all those black

---

[71] vieux Zaffaire (French Creole) - Old business

people from Zaire, Zambia, Zumbulu … why wasn't this concert held in New Zeland? No one has seen black people like this, No one!"

Mitch, the Zambian trained White House Zookeeper must release the wild Zebras, to Zig, Zog, Zabat, Zabello him, and share it on Zoom. Zip your lip, U damm Zombie!

When told by ZNN's Zara Zinga that Z was the 26th letter of the alphabet, he's like. "The alphabet has 26 letters? Nobody knew that, nobody knew." Producer Zoey Zachary had to cut to an extended Zima at Zippys commercial.

Bye folks, Zigning off!

Acknowledgments

We wish to thank in a special way our sister Marvlyn, who contributed to our book; our friend Cliff, who gave some zingers; and Rafael, who did all the graphics and editing, bringing our book to life. Thanks for your patience and understanding and helping to make this possible.

About the Author

Adele, Bentworth, and Ceci James are siblings who were born and raised in Dominica together with five other siblings where they learned the value of reading, staying informed, and being funny. Today, all three siblings live in New York and enjoy communicating daily with their other siblings who live Aruba, Dominica, Holland, and the UK.

CPSIA information can be obtained
at www.ICGtesting.com
Printed in the USA
LVHW041634291120
672964LV00018B/706